A WORK IN PROGRESS

STORIES & POEMS & MEMOIR

JON EEKHOFF

DEDICATION

To Cheryl, Dylan, and Emma

"How vain it is to sit down to write
when you have not stood up to live."

Henry David Thoreau

CONTENTS

PREFACE

By the Editors
Heidi Hansen and Linda B. Myers

A Work in Progress is a collection of short stories, memoirs, and poems by Jon Eekhoff. Jon created all of these works in the years before suffering a Traumatic Brain Injury on March 17, 2018. Because we were members of his writers critique group, as well as the founders of Olympic Peninsula Authors, Jon asked us if we would help him compile his collection.

Our role has been to aid Jon in bringing these stories to you. After his fall, Jon lost touch with the brilliance you will see on display here. In the two years since, he has learned to speak and read again. He is beginning to compose new works. We are astounded by his progress; his potential appears boundless to us.

We are both honored and humbled to have been cheering from the stands while Jon fights for the victory of his life.

INTRODUCTION
By members of the Eekhoff family

Saturday, March 17, 2018

"Jon's fallen off the roof. We're headed to the hospital in Port Angeles." With that message from his wife Cheryl, life for this family changed forever. That day they entered 'The Waiting Room' figuratively and realistically to grieve, accept, and weather whatever those changes would be.

For fifty-three years, Jon's brain was trained to be creative, expressive, off-the-wall hilarious, bizarre, weird, loving, contemplative, committed, compassionate, and an inspiration to students, friends, and family alike. Then, just like that, his life was interrupted.

Recovery from Traumatic Brain Injury is a non-linear emotional and physical rollercoaster. Jon, with Cheryl at his side, faced months of surgery, eye and memory clinics, as well as physical, vocational, and recreational therapy. They continue to face the long, arduous challenge of speech therapy at the University of Washington. Today, Jon has moved beyond the irate word salad of the early days to a man whose wit still sparkles, whose spirit is that of an athlete with a dogged determination to succeed, and a belief he will teach again.

Jon always defined himself as a writer. The stories, memoirs and poems in this book reflect his childhood, his school and teaching years, his boundless imagination as a storyteller. The creative spirit behind them is still the same Jon. For him, growth is no longer only about recovery. It's about who he will be more than who he was. Jon faces a future without boundaries, where each day is a work in progress.

Here is his story in his own words, as well as the words of his family.

————

Jon's Journey: Falling and Rising
By Jon's father, Dave Eekhoff

There are things that happen in life that wound the best of us. Some wounds are visible, others not so much. We all survive our wounds, but the secret to becoming resilient when wounded is how our wounds are cared for.

Mid-March 2018, St. Patrick's Day to be exact, we received a phone call...the one you never want to get. It was Cheryl. "Jon's fallen off the roof," or something to that effect. It's hard to have historically accurate recall of something so life changing. The day was compressed into frantic travel to Olympic Memorial Hospital in Port Angeles, where Jon was rushed by ambulance...then back home and picking up Cheryl...then to Harborview Medical Center in Seattle where Jon had been medivacked by helicopter. The trauma center there is the best.

Business was attended to during our drive to Seattle. Cheryl talked to hospital personnel to give permission for life saving surgery, a craniectomy to gain access to a brain that wanted to swell more than Jon's head would allow. It saved his life.

Once at Harborview, Cheryl, Geri and I were at the mercy of Jon's ability to stay alive, let alone recover in those early hours. When the most critical moments passed it seemed as though time slowed down. As we settled into an unfamiliar but soon to be usual routine, we became acquainted with the staff of doctors, nurses, interns, custodians, and other people whose very presence surrounded us with care. We knew we were in the right place. Jon's wounds and ours were being cared for and that, I have discovered, is the most important thing for this long journey of healing.

Anyone who has been through an ordeal like this will understand when I say, "Falling is easy… it is rising after the fall that is hard." I remember an older doctor, probably an emeritus doc, who had seen a lot and been with many families over the years, whose wisdom seemed brittle in the moment, but the truth of his words is now part of our experience. "We know how to keep people alive, but we can't guarantee how their life will turn out."

The most helpful thing about this journey with Jon and Cheryl is the recognition that we can't expect to go back to the way things were before the fall, nor maybe would we want to. But because of the fall, a new opportunity for finding out what we are made of and made for comes to light. Jon's fall has challenged us all to realize how thin the line is between here and there. And so, we rise…!

With special memories forever etched into my life, I respectfully offer this reflection.

The Call That Changed March 17, 2018
By Jon's mother, Geri Eekhoff

Jon has always been the kid in the family to have the most doctor's trips growing up. His delivery should have predicted his life would be a challenge, for he was born with the umbilical cord wrapped around his neck.

When he was about a year old, he fell off our bed and broke his left leg. He was in a cast for six weeks, with several repairs to the cast (Chicago).

His head has experienced most of the trauma. Around two years old, he ran headlong into a display about copper mining that was jutting out of a deck area. At three, his sister pushed the swing into the center of his forehead. When he was about five, he decided he could fly and jumped from one camp bunk to another, again hitting the same area of his forehead. Each time these incidents meant a trip to the doctor for stitches.

His high school senior year, Jon broke his wrist playing basketball outside our house, and then, as an adult, had surgery on his left hand due to a basketball injury. Jon also had two truck accidents that he walked away from. So you might say, we have had some preparation for "another accident."

But!

We were not prepared for our teacher son to fall off a roof, a two-story roof at that! When Cheryl called, we stopped everything and headed to Port Angeles where the ambulance was taking Jon. Once there, the Doogie Howser-looking doctor in the ER informed us Jon needed to be airlifted to

Harborview Hospital. They would need to intubate him before flying. It was serious. His brain was already swelling.

We returned home to grab clothes and medications for whatever lay ahead. We met up with Cheryl and while on the ferry to Seattle, she received several calls from Harborview doctors. They were already taking Jon to surgery for a craniectomy and needed her permission. Once we were at Harborview, waiting seemed interminable. My mind went through a million scenes of what could be the outcome for Jon. We watched the sign to let us know: 728 in surgery...728 out of surgery...728 in recovery.

Finally, Dr. White came out to let us know that Jon would be in the Trauma Intensive Care area on the ninth floor. Jon was on constant monitoring including neurological checks. It was difficult to see "**NO BONE**" written on his scalp where there was no scalp bone. Above his bed was "**WEAR HELMET**" when out of bed. Would he ever be out of his bed? No one knew at this point. Dr. Ramport, Neurosurgeon, showed us the area on the computer that was affected—Jon's speech and language area—the most important area of the brain for an English teacher.

On the thirteenth day, Jon clearly stated, "Mom, I am sore." Those were glorious hopeful words to hear. Jon is a walking miracle for he not only had the TBI but fractures of the ribs, left ankle, right clavicle, left scapula, and thoracic fracture. Fortunately, by the time he was able to walk, these had all healed.

March 17, 2018 indeed was a drastic change to our day. Day by day, we see recovery and continued growth for Jon. I am so grateful and thankful to all who have gone on this journey with us, especially Cheryl, their children, Dylan and

Emma, and our daughters Jennifer and Katharine, along with all the family and friends who have carried us along in prayer when it was difficult and unknown. Your support has been overwhelming.

———

The Life of a Writer's Spouse
By Jon's wife, Cheryl Eekhoff

Just a few years into our marriage, I realized I had heard all of Jon's stories, but that didn't keep him from continuing to share them with me. I should have been relieved when he started the serious writer's habit of sitting down daily to practice his craft. Instead, I was jealous; we had kids, chores to do, places to go...yet he sat there at the kitchen table with his calendar and notes, meticulously mapping out his novel, *Six Summers in Paris*.

I guess I held back because he was inspired to tell what would be an amazing story, and how awful could it be to be married to the author of the next great American novel? This habit did produce an amazing story that blended fiction and history. Though he kept his day job, teaching high school English, he thought and behaved like an inspired writer...after all, he was always just twenty-four hours away from his next writing session. He traveled to Paris alone to nail down final details, continued to write short stories and poems when inspired; he would even keep a little tablet in the car, and as he was driving, he'd tell me: "Get this down!

Wood whores..." (Reference page 41) or whatever caught his attention at the time.

He would spend a day every spring with a close friend, wandering Powell's Books in Portland, eating good food, and swapping poems. Over the years, letters of inquiry went unanswered or outright rejected. He moved on to other novels, more poems, short stories — just because the muse struck him. He needed to get words down on paper — not for fame and fortune but because he had stories to tell. In his travels, he's continued to add to his story-worthy adventures and even entertained a small group of loyal fans. He has so much to share.

Then he fell. Since his accident and recovery from Traumatic Brain Injury, Jon hasn't been able to write as he used to. It was the first habit he wanted to return to after being sprung from the hospital after eight weeks, but what came out was a simple mess. I tried to intervene, to transcribe, but I don't have his voice. His brain injury has created an ultimately inappropriate joke: ideas full of craft, humor, wit, skill, but locked in a corner of the brain that is no longer attached to the tongue or the pen or the keyboard. What's a writer to do? Well, for now, return to his old writings, revisit those charms, polish them up, and package them for us to read.

We don't know if his old writing voice will ever return, but we strive for growth. I know he has more stories...especially one great one about despair, persistence, and faith.

———

A Work in Progress
By Jon Eekhoff

It's hard to remember everything. Sometimes I don't admit where I've been. But what I try to do is pretend that I am what I used to be. My neighbor, Hillary, found me on the cement and called for help. Two ambulances came. My ladder was on the ground...I had fallen about twenty feet.

They took me to Olympic Medical Center in Port Angeles. The doctors looked at my brain and said it was time to fly me to Harborview in Seattle. I don't remember anything for a month. I might've eaten food, I might've listened to TV, but I don't remember any of it. I recognized this one young lady who seemed like someone that I knew. I wasn't sure what her name was, but after a month I discovered it was my wife, Cheryl. I spent time on the ninth floor, ICU, and on the seventh floor, Acute Care, but I don't remember. When I moved to the fourth floor that's when I began to remember some things. I spent two more months in Harborview. I saw people but it was really rare that I could remember names or read and write anything. TBI (Traumatic Brain Injuries) and aphasia were problems and I decided I could give up or fight through; well here I am.

I was lucky to be alive when I got back to Sequim. I wanted to go back into my old world where I was able to read and write for hours in the morning, then go to work with students. I enjoyed working with Advanced Placement English and with those students who weren't good at reading and writing. I worked with them to become better.

I spent a month pretending that I could still teach, to do all of the things that I used to be able to do. I lied about a lot of things. I wanted to teach, but I had to admit that I could not read or write myself, that I'm not able to do what I used to be able to do. I hope to teach again someday, but what I have to do now is go slowly and re-learn little pieces instead of thinking of big things. I'm a slow old man. I'm okay with that. I need to be in the moment as opposed to thinking of the past and thinking of the future. I've written four novels, and I'm going to finish the last one of those. Thank you for what everyone has done for me. Progress can seem slow and small but it's good.

Superhuman-wonder-structure, Jon

The Ladder

One morning father
fell from a red step-ladder
landing on his head.

I pictured his large
body toppling from the
foremost rung. Twisting

between space and time
trying to control something
he could not control.

Like the boy with wax
wings flying too close to the
sun, he tumbled down.

The red ladder watched
this large man's flight, turning and
striking the cool earth.

Newton might have drawn
some principle about force.
This was no apple

Dropping from a tree,
It was the end of something,
Something much larger.

Editor's Note: Jon wrote the poem, *The Ladder*, after his father's fall from a ladder while hanging Christmas lights. While he was knocked unconscious, he did not suffer any broken bones.

Cut

It was a regular piece of lined notebook paper that the basketball coach taped to the inside of the window in the coaches' office. He posted the list and then disappeared into the back, out of our sight. We crowded around the document like it was a holy relic; at the top of the page the coach had scrawled "Freshman Basketball Players" and then listed thirteen names down the left side of the paper. It was the culmination of two days of try-outs designed to weed out the weak and keep the strong.

I waited behind the crowd of boys who were nearly pressing their faces against the glass to see if they were on the list. When it came to my turn, I looked for my name near the top of the list where I assumed it would be. I scanned the list once, twice, three times and did not see my name. I even pressed my finger against the glass and ran it down the list just to make sure I hadn't missed my name, but it wasn't there. I rode home in silence with my friends, who all made the team. I held my tears for home. That regular piece of lined notebook paper changed my life, changed my feelings about myself, changed who I was, and changed who I would become.

Initially I was angry. I couldn't make sense of why I wasn't selected, and I did what most people in my situation do: I blamed the coach. As my bitterness ebbed over time, I began to think about what it would take to make the team next year. One day, without really knowing why I was doing it, I sat down and wrote out my goals: make the team next year, make varsity my junior year, be the best player on the team as a senior, and make the Fresno City/County All-star team. These goals seemed attainable, these goals seemed realistic, and these goals became the focus of my athletic efforts over the next three years. They drove me.

I signed up for preseason condition with the basketball players the next fall. I was the only person in the class that hadn't been on the team in the previous season. When we ran the stairs in the football stadium, I tried to beat everyone. When we ran 220 sprints, I tried to beat everyone. When we jumped rope, I tried to beat everyone. When we ran two miles, I tried to beat everyone. Everyone else was just working out, getting in shape, but I was there to compete and to win.

When the following year's try-outs were over and the list for the JV team was posted on the glass in the coaches' office my name was there, number 13, the last on the list. I was the last to pick my uniform, I was last off the bench in the games, I was last selected during drills. I was like fungus that wouldn't go away. I kept showing up and kept trying, and eventually I started to get noticed.

By the end of my high school basketball career I had reached all of my goals. It didn't just happen: I learned about beating my competition by outworking my competition. It was a lesson I would use again in college as I worked out each day. Each time my college coach brought in a recruit that played my position, I played like a man possessed. I banged. I fouled. I played dirty. I destroyed my competition. I never stepped on to the court without feeling I was the best player there. I never wanted to give someone the power to tell me I wasn't good enough again.

That little piece of notebook paper, taped to the coaches' window, flashes in my mind occasionally, but it is no longer a painful memory, and it isn't a memory of what I lost by not being on the freshman basketball team. It is a memory of what I gained through rejection. I don't really know what would have happened to me if I made the freshman team, but I am certain that I would have continued floating through life in second gear, hoping to get by on my God-given talents, instead of pushing myself to become better.

It is hard to think about how different my life would be without that little piece of paper. I wouldn't be the person I am today. I wouldn't be as driven. I wouldn't be as focused. I wouldn't be as optimistic about the potential we all hold inside. I wouldn't be who I am today.

Southern Man

James regretted his decision to travel to Paris.

London might have been dirty, old and unorganized, but at least the people spoke a variation of English the family could understand.

The wide-mouthed family French lessons at University of Alabama (Roll Tide) were not helpful in a country where people opened their mouths just a crack. Words came from deep inside French people, compacted and dulled by the time they escaped the mouth. James wondered how anybody could understand what anyone else was saying. James' family was taught to speak with their lips, tongue and teeth, like dogs eating peanut butter. The language James heard coming out of the mouths of the French people sounded like a series of low nasal groans. "PaRDoN, C Voo PlAy?" never got the same response in Paris as it did at the University of Alabama (Roll Tide).

James' family began offending people when they first landed at Heathrow. In a reversal of Sherman's march to the sea, his family managed to burn and pillage just about every historical landmark they visited. Waitresses were subjected to questions about British dentists, complaints were lodged about paying to pee, and history was altered in typical southern fashion. "That is why our ancestors left this country and why God has blessed the USA."

The trip to Paris on the Eurostar started well. Grandpa told his story about saving the French in WWII, Momma told her story about traveling to Paris with her sorority sisters over a spring break, and James told his French jokes. "Why did Hitler plant trees on the Champs d Elysees? Because Germans like to march in the shade." The family had not noticed the train car leaked passengers with each loud story of France. When they arrived in Paris their car was empty except for two backpackers who kept their iPod headphones on the entire trip.

James' family exited the train and bunched together on the platform, blocking traffic. "James, maybe we should just take a taxi to the hotel," Momma said looking around the vast building.

"No, I read the Metro map, and there is a stop right next to our hotel. Taxi drivers in Paris are not the most ethical people in the world."

"How do you know that, Daddy?" James Junior asked.

"Well Junior, the French don't believe in God. They're all Existentialists and Atheists. In my Philosophy class at the University (Roll Tide) I learned that they don't believe in right and wrong; they just do what they want. That's why God punished their country by having Hitler destroy it. If Grandpa here hadn't come over to fight they'd all be speaking German now."

"A taxi would be easier than taking our bags on the train," Momma said. "Grace's bag is so large it might be difficult for her to manage it on the train."

"I can handle it, Momma," Grace said. "I'm sixteen you know."

"You'll always be my little baby, Sweetheart," Momma said putting her arm around Grace.

"We're going to take the train. It will be good for us to get used to using the train, and it won't cost us one hundred Euros to get to the hotel," James said. "Follow me. I looked at a map of the station while we were on the train. The Metro stops are over that way." James used his head to nod in the direction he thought the family should go.

"Daddy, there are more people in here than at the Iron Bowl," Junior said.

"Yes, and the good thing is son, the dumbest Frenchman is twice as smart as the smartest Auburn fan. (Roll Tide)."

"Oh, James you are so funny," Momma said picking her way through the crowd behind her husband. "James, don't go too fast. Your daddy is not going to be able to keep up."

"Don't worry dear, I know my way around Paris," Big Daddy said from the rear.

"Yes, Daddy, but that was a few years ago. I think Paris has changed since WWII."

The family pushed through the crowd in single file moving at an inconsistent pace. James stopped every twenty feet to check his daddy and look for the Metro entrance. "There it is. Right there, the big blue M with the circle around it. That's the entrance."

The mouth of the entrance was wide but clogged with tourists and con men. The white tile entranceway reminded

James of an old-fashioned bathroom. Old people stood there, mouths open, gazing into the distance looking like Alzheimer's had struck them at the most unfortunate moment. Young, dirty backpackers stood dazed by a combination of too many days on the road, too little sleep, and gnawing hunger. The only people moving were the pickpockets and con men. Like rats drawn to food dropped at the fair, these young men moved in and pecked at their prey.

"Do you speak English?" a young lady wearing a black dress and black head covering asked James. She held a small piece of paper with a message.

"Yes, I do," James responded out of habit.

"I need money," she said holding out the piece of paper so James could read it. James stopped and began reading and was swarmed by several other young women in black dresses.

"James, watch out. They are trying to steal your wallet," Momma shouted from behind him.

James snapped out of his "help the world" trance and moved into reptilian mode. "Git away from me," he said swinging his free arm. "Git away." James created just enough commotion to gain notice from the two policemen standing near the entrance. The swarm of women dressed in black melted into the crowd, and James pushed his way into the entrance.

"Daddy, there is a ticket machine here." James Junior pointed to a line of people facing a silver ticket machine on the wall.

"I think we will wait in this line," James said pointing to a roped off area with a long line that snaked around three times before opening to three ticket agents sitting in their glass offices. "This looks like a better choice, son. These people will help us if there is a problem. There's too many people over there."

James knew the ticket machine might look easier, but the crowds of people and swarthy young men offering to help gave him an uneasy feeling, so he waited in line. "Why don't you wait against the wall over there while I get the tickets. Don't talk to anyone and don't help anyone." The line inched forward. Every ten seconds James would check to see if his family was still where he ordered them to stand. They looked defeated standing against the white tile walls. Momma deflected any "help" being offered. James felt her resentment. It was too late to take a taxi, but he knew he would pay for his mistake for at least the rest of the day.

After thirty minutes, James was next in line to be served. He approached the open ticket agent. "Bonjour, I need…sank (James held up five fingers) tickets to Felix Faure." James pushed a twenty Euro note through the bowl-shaped opening.

The black-haired, round-headed agent pushed a few keys on his keyboard, "Oui, your French is very good Monsieur."

"Merci, I have been taking lessons."

"I can tell," the agent said moving the tickets and change through the hole at the bottom of the glass partition. "Bon voyage."

"Merci." James grabbed the tickets and shoved the change into the front pocket of his Khakis. He turned and moved to where he told his family to stand; they were gone. A jolt passed through James. He scanned the crowds, but he could not see his family anywhere.

"Daddy! Daddy! We are over here!" James turned and saw his family pressed against the wall further down the corridor. James cut through the crowd pulling his suitcase.

"Got 'em. Five tickets. The agent said my French was very good," James announced to his wife.

"Great, now all we have to do is get to the hotel. You know a taxi would have dropped us off right at the hotel entrance," Momma said.

"Why did you move? I thought I lost you."

"A couple of those young men were trying to help us. Your daddy gave them the business though."

"I told them the last time I was in France I didn't need a ticket to get around town. I just took an Army jeep and drove where I wanted, and people were happy to see me," Big Daddy said raising his voice so everyone around him could hear.

"So we moved over here."

"I thought Big Daddy was going to fight those guys," Junior said.

"And I would have beat them, too," Big Daddy said.

"Let's keep your fighting limited to wars, Daddy," James said. "Well, everyone ready? I hear the Metro is better than the Tube. Cleaner, bigger and more efficient."

The Metro was cleaner, bigger, and more efficient, but that did not make it easier for novices to navigate. Suitcases got stuck in automated turnstiles, stairs had to be negotiated, train lines had to be selected and reselected, trains were taken in the wrong direction. By the time the family reached Felix Faure a full two hours had passed.

They emerged from the metro tunnels like released prisoners of some Russian gulag. "Daddy, how much further is it to our hotel?" Junior asked.

"It should be right here," James said, scanning the corners for a street sign. He took out his pocket-sized map and tried to orient himself. "Sugar, do you see any street signs? I can't figure out where we are."

"I don't see any signs either. Maybe we should ask those boys," Momma said.

James looked at the two boys skateboarding, hoodlums as far as James could tell, banging their boards against the side of a building again and again in an attempt to do something. "Those boys don't look too helpful. I think it might be this way." James began rolling his suitcase down the longer street. "Whoa, look out for doggie bombs. Oh, my goodness. There are doggie bombs all over the sidewalk. Grace! Grace! What are you doing? Stop staring at those boys and follow your family!"

"This is dis-gus-ting," Momma said. "What kinds of people don't clean up their doggie bombs? Gracie! Get your behind over here right now! Stop looking at those boys! If you want to look at people like that, I will take you to the local prison when we get back home."

"Sorry, Momma. I was just trying to figure out what they were doing."

"They're trying to ruin the side of that building, that's what they are doing," James shouted in an effort to shame the boys into stopping.

"Daddy, you're embarrassing me."

"Your gawking is embarrassing us, Darling," Momma said. "Now git over here."

"Yes, Momma."

"How're you doing, Daddy?" James asked.

"I'm fine. Your wife was right about the taxi though."

"It'll all be okay when we get to the hotel and turn on that A/C. We'll all cool off and then walk to the Eiffel Tower, or we could catch a taxi." James smiled at his wife.

"Yes, some cool air would feel good right now," Momma said.

"Hey, there it is. I see the hotel sign," James said pointing at a red neon sign about halfway down the street. Just as James raised his arm to point out the sign a pigeon flying overhead squirted a stream of waste. The wet droppings fell from the sky and landed in a stream on James' wrist and hand. "Gawl durn it!"

"What is it, Sugar?"

"One of them durn pigeons just dropped a bomb on my arm," James said as he shook off what he could.

"Here you go, Sugar, I have some tissues," Momma said handing over several unused ones.

"Thank you." James did his best to wipe off the mess. "Well, I guess I'll get the rest done once we check in to the hotel."

The family rolled their bags along the walkway toward their hotel. A small burgundy awning popped out over the entrance with a golden script "Hotel Eiffel Tower." James wheeled into the hotel and was struck by the size of the foyer. The online pictures made the front desk and foyer look much larger, but James' family could barely manage to fit themselves and their bags in the little room.

James smiled at the young, dark-haired women behind the counter, "Bonjour. Jee swee un reservation. I have a reservation."

She smiled, "What name?"

"Bridge, James Bridge."

"Oh, I see…" She clicked the keys on the computer in front of her. "Two rooms?"

"Yes, one for my family and one for my Daddy."

She twisted her lips, looking down at the monitor, "I don't…ah…the rooms are not large enough for all," she made a sweeping motion with her arms.

"What? The kids can sleep on cots. We'll make it work."

She twisted her lips again, "A moment," she said and walked back through a burgundy curtain.

"What's goin' on, Sugar?"

"She said the room was too small to fit our family."

"Well, the kids can sleep on cots, did you tell her that?"

"Yes, I did. That's when she left."

"You will not pay for another room. This is a scam, James, and I don't…" Momma cut herself off as the front desk lady returned with an older lady dressed in a blue floral housedress.

"I will take you to the room to show you," the young woman said to James. She moved from behind the desk and escorted James around the corner. "We will take the elevator." James followed noticing her bra straps through her white shirt; he checked her tight black skirt. Yes, there was something about French women.

"Here it is," she said moving her arm to a telephone booth sized elevator.

"That's the elevator? Wow, I have a gun safe bigger than that," James said squeezing into the space. The young woman stepped in forcing James to push his body against the back wall in order to avoid touching her.

"Is this your first time to Paree?" she asked as she closed the folding glass door. She faced the front of the elevator and pushed five.

"Pardon?"

"Paree, is this your first trip?"

"Oh, Paris. Yes, this is my first trip to France. My wife and father have been here before." The elevator began creeping up. James could smell the young lady's perfume. He looked at her short dark hair, her shoulders, her white neck, and felt her body's heat.

"I hope you like Paree." The elevator stopped. She opened the door, walked into the hall, and showed James to his room. "You will see. The rooms are small for your family." She opened the door, and James looked into the smallest hotel room he had ever seen: two cot-sized beds and a large armoire took up 90% of the floor space.

"Wow. You're right. We won't all fit in here. Is there a bigger room?"

"No, but we can give you rooms…how do you say it? Together."

"Can I look at them? Are they bigger?"

"They are not bigger. The rooms are together," she said weaving her fingers together. "They are up, on the last floor."

"Okay, I guess we'll do that. It isn't like we have many options. Yes, let's do that. We just want to get settled and turn on some A/C."

The elevator ride back down was slow. James stood behind the girl staring at a small black mole on her neck. He wondered about her body and whether she was one of those free-love European women. For a moment he wished he was in Paris by himself where a small dirty room didn't matter, and he was free to ask young women if they wanted to be kissed.

When the elevator stopped James wanted to stay inside, nevertheless he followed the young woman around the corner and to the small front desk.

"Well, it looks like we will need three rooms," James said to his wife before she could open her mouth. "She will get us adjoining rooms so it will be like one big room."

James' wife made her pouting mouth and crossed her arms, "Not exactly the romantic trip to Paris I imagined."

"Once we get in the rooms and turn on the A/C and get rested everyone will have a better attitude. You'll see." James moved to the front desk, handed over his credit card, signed the papers without looking at the cost, and took the keys. "Junior, you are going to love this elevator. It is the size of a shower."

It took four elevator rides to get James' family and their bags to the stale air of the sixth floor. The heat in the hallway was oppressive, even for Southerners. James sweated through his crimson Alabama (Roll Tide) golf shirt in a matter of two elevator rides, and by the time he moved all the bags and stashed all the members of his family, he was ready for an afternoon nap with the A/C set on high. Unfortunately there was no air conditioning in the Hotel Eiffel Tower.

***

Luna lived in Paris. Really she lived around Paris, never the same place for long, but she always worked in Paris. Sometimes she worked around the Eiffel Tower, other days she stood outside Notre Dame, and occasionally she worked the large Metro stations. Each location called upon a different set of job skills. She worked the Tower with her younger sisters in a large pack, Notre Dame was most often a place she worked with her older sisters, and she worked the Metro with her cousin, Camlo, and her sister closest in age, Mala. She liked the Metro best. Sometimes her cousin would convince the team to try the streets and ATMs outside of the major tourist areas, but that was much riskier.

It was not a good living, but it was a living. There were a few times when she got caught, but she was proud of her strength and talent.

It had already been a long day when she saw him a block from the ATM and followed. It was too late for him to be out by himself in this neighborhood. She signaled her sister, Mala, across the street, who then waved down the street to her cousin, Camlo. Camlo signaled and began moving toward the man in the red shirt, an American, they could tell.

Camlo jogged toward the green BNP Paribas ATM and pretended to pull a card from his back pocket. The trio had already placed a piece of black tape across the ATM camera lens. They hoped a drunk Frenchman would come along, but a sober American was just as good.

Camlo had grown up working the three-card con game in Berlin, so making it look like he was using the ATM was an effortless bit of movement. He pushed his right shoulder up against the ATM's privacy shield as he felt the man in the red shirt get closer. He heard the man stop walking. Camlo played with the keys for a moment longer and then mimed pulling out cash and put an empty hand into his front pocket. He knew the longer he could make the man wait the easier the next part would be.

Camlo took a peek at the man over his shoulder and then pretended to pull out his card and terminate his business at the ATM. He could feel the man's impatience growing. Camlo turned away from the man and took a few steps away from the machine. He lit a cigarette and turned so he could see the man's progress at the ATM. He waited and then pulled the cigarette from his mouth and blew a long stream of smoke into the air. Luna saw the signal and moved. Her sister dashed across the street without a sound and the two women approached the American from behind at the same moment. Luna was first; she pushed her right hand onto the keypad. He shouted, "Hey, gawl durn it," and turned to see who was trying to grab his money. As he turned to his right, Mala reached around and grabbed the Euros as they emerged from the belly of the machine. James didn't see her grab the money, but he saw a girl dressed in black jump between the parked cars and start running across the street. The other girl followed. James acted on instinct and bolted after the girls. His younger days of chasing running backs down in Allgood, Alabama, hopped into his mind. His nickname "Rabbit" had followed him all the way to the University (Roll Tide), and he wasn't about to let some fifteen-year-old girls outrun him.

His Sperry Topsiders slapped against the cobbled street as he chased. He was not an elegant runner. His nickname had more to do with the choppy inconsistency of his stride than with speed, but he was closing in on the girls.

As they ran down the center of the street James shouted, "Stop them. Robbers!" several times, but no one was around to hear him. The girls turned a corner and began laughing. Usually the drunks they robbed would stop running after one hundred meters, but this crazy man in the red shirt was not going to let them get away. As he got closer to them Mala peeled off two twenty Euro notes and dropped them. Ten feet further she dropped two more notes.

James was finished; the pain in his right knee stabbed at him with each step, and he could no longer keep up. The girls began pulling away. James slowed to a jog and watched the girls disappear into the night. He turned and went back to locate the dropped currency.

James felt a wave of relief hit him. The four bills were still in the middle of the road right where they had been dropped. He counted them; he had recovered eighty of the two hundred he requested from the machine, so it wasn't a total loss. The hundred and twenty Euros could be replaced and might not even be missed. James had plenty of money saved for his vacation. He decided not to mention his midnight run and loss of money to his wife. He would just go back to the hotel and slide into bed without a noise.

James didn't feel sick until he got within a few feet of the green ATM. The welcome screen of the machine greeted him: "Bienvenue. Veuillez entrer votre code secret." James pushed the red cancel button several times. Nothing happened. He staggered for a moment, put his hand against the wall, and began hyperventilating. He thought back to the day he called his bank and asked to increase the amount he could take out of an ATM in any twenty-four-hour period. "Stupid, stupid, stupid!" he shouted into the wall. He replayed the whole event in his head. The guy, the guy with the cigarette, he was the one who took the card.

By the time James finished his run and returned to the ATM, Camlo had already called the card numbers to his family camped on the outskirts of Paris. The family passed the number to the rest of the clan, and before James figured out what had happened a flurry of online orders went out: three leather jackets from Prague, four designer handbags from London, handfuls of jewelry from multiple locations, twenty X-box games from Thailand, and twelve black dresses from Milan. The spike in activity was noticed and an email was sent out: "Dear Sir or Madam, Please call our 800 number during business hours. Due to unusual activity on your card, we have placed a hold on further purchases on your credit." The notice didn't inform James that his account now held $189.23.

James spent the next two days of his vacation on the phone. The family spent the days watching French television and complaining about the heat. No one wanted to venture out onto the dangerous streets of Paris. Big Daddy stopped telling war stories. They ate all their meals at a nearby McDonalds. The family took a taxi to the airport and flew out of Paris two days earlier than planned.

James never returned to Paris but did make the Iron Bowl every year (Roll Tide).

JON EEKHOFF

Sunday Morning on the Paris Metro

Was he John preparing the way?
Coming dressed not in camel hair,
but the dusty clothing of the Boulevards.
Flaming hair licking his scalp
as this mad prophet raged
against a mute world,
ruthlessly attacking the crowded,
disinterested congregation.
Shaking a worn Book at this silent mass
he moved from behind his imagined pulpit,
passing between the Metro pews,
and confronted a trio of schoolgirls.
They retreated as he railed in mysterious tongues,
shaking his mighty fist intensely.
They huddled and withstood his windy attack and then—
exited with him at Saint-Michel.

A young woman,
in an emerald sun dress,
stood, firmly pressing her forehead
against the closed Metro doors.
Her blossoms blew in the breeze
exhaled by the tunnel.
Rocking rhythmically, she rolled
her forehead against the cool glass.
Straight blonde hair hung
over her face obscuring a lost expression.
Her eyes darted below to black tracks,
as her slender neck strained to hold her burden.

A seductress, dressed as blackest night,
bit a green apple as she stepped
onto the illuminated train.
Leaning against the cold steel pole,
she twisted with the jostling
car as it pounded down the tracks.
Her red lips parted again allowing the apple's
white flesh to enter that forbidden place,
planting a festering garden of desire
 in men's minds.
These burning gardens spilled their
overgrown buds beyond thought.

Where had our mad prophet gone?
His magic powers were needed.
Could he gather up dust from the tunnel,
combine it with saliva and make a
soothing balm to heal our open wounds?

Travel Pants

I don't know how many times I have thought something was cool and fashionable only to find out later that there really was nothing cool or fashionable about it. I could travel back into my past and discuss the use of purple Toughskin jeans or getting my hair permed, but those were mistakes of an undeveloped brain and excusable. Well, there really isn't an excuse for getting my hair permed, then deciding that it looked better if I didn't comb it.

As I get older, I am less concerned with fashion or trying to fit in. That is the only excuse I can come up with for purchasing and wearing travel pants. You no doubt have seen this variety of pants: lots of pockets, zip off pant legs, and usually some puke-like color. I saw some at REI a number of years back and decided that I must have them. I imagined myself tramping around the world with my handy pants ready for any weather. For some reason, I thought I would look competent and worldly if I had a pair of travel pants. Little did I realize that travel pants actually send out the opposite message to the world: here is a person who can't even figure out if he needs shorts or pants today.

Other than making you look like a dork, travel pants are really handy. Mine had a great little security pocket with a

Velcro flap and a hidden zipper that was just big enough to fit a couple credit cards and a travel pass. If I had been traveling in Africa I would have just needed a Safari hat and travel shirt, and I would have looked like some great white hunter. But I wasn't in Africa. I was in Paris where I looked like an American tourist who dressed for the wrong Hemingway novel.

I was not completely oblivious to my dorkaliciousness. I realized that I looked like a large child whose parents dressed him for the day, but I didn't really care. I was in Paris by myself, staying in a hotel room about the size of an American elevator so I tried to spend my time outside wandering the streets. Unfortunately, it was August, and believe it or not, August is the rainiest month in Paris. I spent a good deal of time walking in the rain like Gene Kelly. That is, if Gene Kelly wore travel pants.

I decided one day to go out to La Defense since I had not been there before and because Matt Damon went there in one of the Bourne movies. I am not completely obsessed with being a spy; it just seems that way to everyone who knows me. Anyway, I took a Metro train packed with business people out to my destination and then proceeded to wander around aimlessly. I am a master of wandering, both purposeful and accidental.

I had some coffee, bought an English language newspaper, watched people and wondered how long it would take me to walk all the way back to my hotel. The sky looked clear, it was still early, and I had nothing else on my list of things to do, so I started walking back toward my hotel.

As I crossed a bridge over the Seine, it started to sprinkle. The light rain didn't really bother me, so I continued on my journey. I stopped and looked at the island where Seurat painted *Le Grande Jatte* and was completely unimpressed. It is still one of my favorite paintings, but the island looked a bit worn and disregarded. That is one of the problems with Paris: it has too much great stuff, too much famous stuff. Some of it is bound to be forgotten. If Seurat had painted a famous painting of an island in the US, someone would have come along and put up wooden cut-outs (the type where you put your head through a hole) so you could take a picture of what you would have looked like in *Le Grande Jatte.* I would bet that most Parisians don't even know that the island exists because they are walking past the place where Lady Di was killed, or where Marie Antoinette was beheaded. That kind of history is tough to compete with.

Anyway, I continued walking, and it started raining a bit harder. I am not made of sugar, so a little water isn't going to melt me, but I live in the Pacific Northwest where we pride ourselves on never carrying umbrellas. A person with an umbrella in Seattle is like a man wearing travel pants in Paris: a tourist. Normally I would put on my raincoat and keep walking, but my raincoat was hanging in a closet in the state of Washington because IT WAS AUGUST, and it isn't supposed to rain in August.

I kept going thinking that I would find a little café, sit down, have a light lunch and wait for the rain to float by. I saw a café and headed for a landing. I took a look at the menu and decided to see how much cash I had on me. I flipped open the Velcro flap on my pants and grabbed the security zipper and gave it a tug. At first I thought it was my cold hands and the possibility that I was in a little bit of a hurry, but once I concentrated on trying to open my security pocket, I realized that the pocket was truly secure. I would not be getting my cash anytime soon. The zipper was stuck. I considered the possibility of pulling with all my might and ripping the pocket open, but I hadn't reached that point of desperation yet. So, I kept walking.

One of the beautiful things about Paris is that the Metro system has stations everywhere, so I figured I would just abandon my walk and take the train back to my hotel. I saw a Metro entrance and proceeded down the stairs, out of the rain. This is where I had another realization: my Metro pass was in my security pocket. So, I did what any normal, adult would do. I found a bench by the entrance and started really tugging at the stuck zipper. At this point, I didn't care if I ripped my pants. I could always buy new travel pants in Paris. There was probably a store called "Pants for Idiots."

I tugged and tugged at the zipper. Man, was it secure.

I hadn't considered what I might look like to people passing by, but when a mother grabbed her son and pulled him away from where I was sitting, I had a mini-epiphany: I am soaked, sitting on a Metro bench, furiously pulling on a zipper located relatively close to my groin, and making noises that could be mistaken for either frustration or ecstasy. I am no Puritan, but public masturbation is something that I imagine even Parisians are against. If I was in a Metro stop near Pigalle my activities probably would have gone unnoticed, or I might have had someone offer to help me, but I wasn't near Pigalle. I sat up and re-evaluated my situation. I could sit here and continue pulling on my pants, disturbing anyone walking by, or I could head back out into the rain and continue my walk.

The walk back to my hotel was long, wet, and long. Did I mention it was a long walk? Well, it was a long walk, so long that when I got to my hotel, my shoes were completely soaked, the kind of soaked where each step makes a squishing noise as water leaks out.

The nice thing about my security pants was that once I took them off in my hotel room, the zipper worked perfectly. There didn't appear to be anything stuck or malfunctioning, so I didn't need to find a store to buy new travel pants.

Flag of Our Neighbors

"You sure you don't want a lawyer?"

"Yeah."

"Okay, I'm going to record this conversation. Today is May 15, 2013 and this is an interview with Andrew Kerr. Would you spell your name for the record?"

"A-n-d-r-e-w K-e-r-r."

"Andrew, you know I am recording this conversation?"

"Yes."

"Andrew, you have chosen to forego legal representation?"

"Huh?"

"You have decided not to have a lawyer representing you during this interview?"

"Yes. I haven't done anything wrong. I don't need a lawyer."

"Okay. So, Mr. Kerr, tell me how did all of this happen?"

"All of what?"

"Mr. Kerr, you know why you are here don't you?"

"Yes."

"Then why don't you tell me how you ended up here today. Start at the very beginning."

"The very beginning...One day I was driving to work, and I saw one of my neighbors was flying a Confederate Flag and one of those Don't Tread On Me ones. I thought it was offensive."

"Did you know this neighbor?"

"I didn't know who lived there. I just drove by the house on my way to work. I thought the people living there were probably red necks, and this confirmed it."

"What made you think they were 'red necks,' as you put it, before you saw the flags?"

"They had about fifteen cars in their front yard."

"When you say fifteen cars you are exaggerating aren't you?"

"A little. There were always four or five cars half taken apart all over the yard."

"Four or five?"

"Yep."

"So what day was the first time you saw the flags?"

"Middle of March probably."

"Then what happened?"

"It bothered me. I went to work, and I couldn't get it out of my mind."

"Where do you work?"

"On an organic farm."

"And what do you do on the farm?"

"I help with the website and deliver fresh vegetables to restaurants in Seattle."

"So these flags bothered you?"

"Yes. Don't they bother you? They should. What kind of moron puts up a Confederate Flag in Sequim? This isn't 1850.

Why doesn't he just put a big neon sign outside his house that says, 'I'm a racist?'"

"There is free speech in the United States."

"There are laws preventing hate speech, too. Nobody seems to remember that do they?"

"So, what did you do after you saw the flag?'

"Well, like I said, I went to work, but it bothered me all day. I talked to a couple of people at work, and they said I should go and talk to the homeowner."

"So, did you do that?"

"Yeah, well kinda. I stopped by after work and went up to the house and knocked on the door."

"What was your intention?"

"I wanted the homeowner to take the flags down."

"Okay. So what happened?"

"Well, I knocked, and it took a long time for anyone to come to the door. I thought maybe nobody heard me knock so, the doorway had one of those metal doors, so there were two doors, you know, like a metal cage door and then a regular wooden one?"

"I know what you mean."

"So, I thought maybe they didn't hear me knock on the metal door, so I started to open that one so I could knock on the wooden door. I guess there was some an alarm on the door, because as soon as I opened it the thing went off. That's when I saw Mr. Taylor."

"Where was he?"

"He was in the house. He had opened the inside door. It probably looked like I was trying to run away but I wasn't."

"But it probably looked like you were running away."

"Yeah, that's what I said, but I was just trying to get away from the noise."

"I understand, but you can understand Mr. Taylor's concern. This neighborhood has had a number of break-ins recently."

"Yeah, I know. I live close by."

"Describe Mr. Taylor."

"He was in his wheelchair, well, one of those scooter things, not a real wheelchair. He had a big gun sitting on his lap, and he looked like he was about 400 years old."

"What kind of gun?"

"A big one. One of those long ones."

"A shotgun?"

"I guess. What is the difference between a shotgun and a rifle?"

"A shotgun shoots shells and a rifle shoots bullets. Shotguns have larger barrels."

"Then it must have been a shotgun."

"Okay, what happened next?"

"The alarm was off, so I walked toward the door, and before I could say anything he raised the gun off his lap and pointed it at me. He said, 'I can shoot intruders.'"

"Ever have a gun pointed at you before?"

"No."

"Scary huh?"

"Yeah."

"Then what happened?"

"I put my arms up and said, 'I'm sorry for setting off the alarm. I just wanted to talk to you.'"

"Did he put his gun down?"

"No, he said he could shoot me since I tried to enter his house, and the law was on his side. He was pretty angry."

"Then what happened?"

"I talked to him about the flags."

"What do you remember about the conversation?"

"I remember he wasn't happy with me, and he wasn't going to take down his flags."

"Do you remember any details of the conversation?"

"I remember he kept saying, 'My son died in Vietnam to protect your freedoms' or something like that, and he kept calling me boy. 'My son died in Vietnam to protect your freedoms, boy.'"

"What did you say?"

"I said I thought Vietnam was a conflict we should have avoided, and I was sorry his son died in a stupid war."

"You said that?"

"Yeah. He said he should shoot me for thinking like that."

"Like what?"

"Good question. I guess for thinking Vietnam was stupid. He'd have to shoot a lot of people if he was going to shoot everyone who thought Vietnam was stupid."

"Did you say that?"

"No. I didn't think talking about Vietnam was getting me anywhere, so I tried to change the subject back to the flags."

"Were you able to get back to the flags?"

"Sort of. I was able to mention the flags being offensive, but he kept saying he had his First and Second Amendment rights. Each time he said Second Amendment he would pat his gun. He wasn't listening, he kept on with the Vietnam, freedoms, and First Amendment stuff until I said none of what he was saying made sense."

"You said that?"

"Yes, I can't stand the stupid argument that wars fought in other countries protect my right to fly a Confederate flag. That's just stupid. Take Iraq for instance. How does my freedom get protected by our soldiers fighting in the Middle East?"

"They're fighting the terrorists over there so that we don't have to fight them here."

"That's what they want you to think."

"Who are they?"

"The Feds, the military industrial complex, the oil companies…it has nothing to do with freedom. It is all about money."

"I think we might disagree about that one."

"We don't have to agree."

"That's right. It's a free country."

"Sort of."

"Back to the conversation, what happened?"

"Well, he kept getting madder and madder, and he wouldn't listen to anything I was saying. I decided I was wasting my time, so I did my best to end the conversation and leave."

"What was stopping you?"

"He started calling me names and trying to provoke me."

"How? What was he saying?"

"Oh, he called me a Communist, a Socialist, Obama lover, and a Nazi."

"A Nazi?"

"Yeah, I have no idea why?"

"Maybe because you were trying to infringe on his freedom of speech."

"You know, that annoys me. I'm not the guy who put up a Confederate flag. What if I started passing out blankets with smallpox to Indians, and saying it was my heritage, and I wanted to honor my forefathers?"

"Huh?"

"Okay, bad example, but you know Confederate flags are offensive. I mean we don't let people burn crosses in yards and march around in KKK outfits. If your neighbor started burning crosses in his yard every night you would say something wouldn't you? It is 2013."

"I might. So what happened next?"

"I gave up. I told him I was going to call the police and report him. He told me to hurry up and call because he was going to call the police also and report me for breaking and entering. At that point I figured it was best to leave."

"Is that when you first contacted us?'

"Yes. I called and reported the flags."

"Do you remember who you talked to?"

"No, I just called and filed a complaint. I knew nobody was going to do anything."

"It is his property. Is that when you decide to take things into your own hands?"

"Hold on. I didn't take things into my own hands. I waited for about a week to see if you guys were going to do anything."

"It says here that you filed a report on March 30, and then Mr. Taylor reported the theft of his flags on April 1."

"What are you saying?"

"You said you waited a week. It sounds like you waited for two days, or one day and two nights, not a week."

"I guess. What difference does it make?"

"It makes a difference. Why didn't you admit to taking the flags when you were first asked about them?"

"How do you know I took them?"

"We found them in the back of your Prius."

"Okay."

"When the police came to your house to ask you about the flags you said you didn't know what they were talking about."

"I guess."

"That's what the incident report says. It also says that you claimed that it was probably an April Fool's joke."

"I remember that."

"Why didn't you admit to taking the flags?"

"I don't know. I didn't want to get in trouble. I don't usually go around stealing flags."

"So you admit taking Mr. Taylor's flags?"

"I took his flags. Yes, I took the racist's flags."

"Did you do that at night?"

"Yes."

"Do you want to tell me about it?"

"Not really."

"Do you want a lawyer now?"

"No, I don't want a lawyer for stealing two $10 flags."

"Okay, tell me how you did it."

"I dressed in black, walked over there and cut the flags down."

"Did you use a knife?"

"I wouldn't use a good knife on that. I used some old scissors."

"Did you think that was the end of it?"

"I did."

"Then what happened?"

"Well, for about two weeks there was no flag."

"That make you happy?"

"I don't know about happy, but it was good not to see that crap every morning and evening."

"Then what happened?"

"One day I see he has a new flag up."

"What kind of flag was it this time?"

"Another type of Confederate flag, but with a gun on it. So I went home and Googled: Confederate Flag + Gun, and there it was."

"Describe what you found."

"It was a Confederate flag with an assault rifle. On the bottom it said, 'Come and Get it.' I have no idea who sells this crap. Who sits at home and thinks, 'You know what this Confederate flag needs? It needs a big gun and a stupid saying.'"

"Have you ever been to the South, Mr. Kerr?"

"No."

"It's different there."

"Another good reason to stay away."

"Then what happened?"

"Well, I thought about calling the police."

"Because you were afraid we'd find out you stole the other flags?"

"No, because you guys didn't do anything the first time. I wasn't worried about getting caught. I thought it was the right thing to do."

"Then why not admit you stole the flags when you were questioned?"

"I didn't want to get in trouble."

"Okay, so you didn't call us. Is this when you decided to take the law into your own hands?"

"I wasn't taking the law anywhere, I just figured I would head back there at night and cut it down."

"Is that what you did?"

"That was the plan, but he had installed a big motion detector light, like a spotlight, so as soon as I got close to his yard the whole place lit up like Times Square. So I hid back in the trees for a little bit and then walked home and got my monocular."

"Monocular?"

"It is like a binocular with one tube."

"Tube?"

"The round thing with the glass in it. The thing you look through."

"The lens?"

"Yeah, the lens. I got my monocular and looked at the situation. He had four new lights in different parts of the front yard, and then I noticed the flag didn't have a string running all the way to the ground."

"What do you mean?"

"The string holding up the flag, it was tied way, way up there. Close to the top of the pole. He must have used a thirty-foot ladder to get that all the way up there."

"Is that when you decided to cut the flagpole down?"

"No, I wasn't sure what to do, so I went home and thought about it. It took me a few days to decide what to do. I figured if I got up real early in the morning I could unscrew the light bulbs from the motion lights, and nobody would notice, and then I could come back at night and try something different."

"Is that what you did?"

"Yep, I got up early, rode my bike over there and unscrewed the bulbs."

"They weren't high up?"

"Nope, I could reach all four of them by standing on a folding chair."

"Did you bring a folding chair with you?"

"No, I rode my bike. I took the chair from the side of his house."

"Then what did you do?"

"I checked out the pole real quick and left."

"What do you mean 'checked out the pole?'"

"I wanted to see what it was made of and how big around it was."

"And?"

"It was metal and about four inches thick."

"Then what happened?"

"I went to work. I talked to a guy who knew how to cut down trees. I figured he could give me some good advice about how to cut down the pole."

"Did you tell him you were going to cut down a pole?"

"No, I told him I had a tree to cut down that I wanted to fall a certain direction. He gave some good advice. He even offered to do it himself. He said to tie the tree off with a thick rope to something solid so I could pull the tree the right direction."

"And then what did you do?"

"I went to Home Depot and got some rope and talked to a guy about how to cut through a metal pipe. He gave me a handsaw, but he really thought I should use a power saw. I told him I couldn't make noise because my neighbors. So I took the saw and rope and headed home."

"At any point did you think this had gotten a little out of control?"

"No, it seemed pretty simple, wait until dark, tie the pole off to my car bumper, cut the pole, and drive away."

"No, I mean all the things you were doing to get Mr. Taylor's flag down. Didn't it seem like a lot of work?"

"Somebody had to do something."

"Ever consider talking to his neighbors?"

"People like Mr. Taylor aren't going to listen to anyone unless they are on Fox News."

"So what went wrong?"

"I started sawing."

"You tied the pole off to your car?"

"Yep."

"What time of night was this?"

"Around one."

"So, you tied it off and started sawing?"

"Yep, but it was really slow. The pole was filled with cement and the saw couldn't cut through it. So I tried to cut all the way around the metal."

"Explain that more clearly."

"I thought I could cut all the metal and then push the pole over."

"How'd that work?"

"It seemed like it was working, but I couldn't push the pole over."

"Is that when you decided to pull the pole down with your car?"

"Yep."

"What went wrong?"

"Well, I probably should have tied the rope up higher, and then there was Mr. Taylor waking up or whatever."

"When were you first aware that Mr. Taylor was awake?"

"I saw a light go on in the house."

"Where were you?"

"In my car."

"Then what happened?"

"Mr. Taylor comes rolling out of the house in his scooter with his shotgun. I got scared and floored it."

"The pole broke?"

"I guess. I just floored it and heard a big crash."

"How far did you drag the pole before you stopped and untied the rope?"

"About a block."

"What were you thinking?"

"I saw the pole smashed a couple cars on the street and caused a lot of damage."

"But you didn't notice the pole struck Mr. Taylor?"

"No, absolutely not. I wouldn't have driven away if I knew the pole hit him."

"But you were okay driving away after causing thousands of dollars' worth of damage to six of your neighbor's cars?"

"I was scared."

"When did you first hear Mr. Taylor was killed by the pole?"

"He wasn't killed by the pole. The pole hit his leg."

"He had a heart attack."

"People have heart attacks all the time."

"You don't think you're responsible for the heart attack?"

"Are you kidding me? Mr. Taylor is responsible for his own heart attack. You're not hanging that one on me."

"When did you realize the pole had struck Mr. Taylor?"

"When you came to my house…you know what? I do want a lawyer. Turn that off."

"Okay."

Outside Westhaven State Park

Wood Whores
Lingering on the corner.
Eying each other lustfully.
Merchandise bound tightly.

Dry wood $5.00
Hand painted signs read.
City campers
Prowl by, leaning out
Their truck windows,
Leering at the bundles
Piled high in back
Of dilapidated 30-year-old
Pick-ups.

Salesmen dressed as Tom Joad
Sit sprawled out in 5-year-old
Aluminum chairs, smoking generic
Cigarettes with a come hither
Look, hidden beneath greasy
Baseball caps.

City folk roughing it for the weekend,
Meet their country neighbors,
Capitalism Westport style.

America the Beautiful.

Tell Me A Scary Story

"Tell me a story," a tiny voice came from the back of the car one evening.

Because we lived in such a rural area, our family often had long drives home from the city on weekend evenings. We listened to the radio until my children became bored and wanted a story. I had all but exhausted all the G and PG stories about my childhood and did not want to wander into the R rated material until my children were well on their way out of college and had their first jobs.

"Is there a type of story you want?"

"Tell me a scary story," Dylan said before Emma had a chance to express an opinion.

Now, a mature adult would tell young children a scary story about a windstorm and a tree brushing a window, or a story about a dark hallway, but my children have only one mature adult in their family, and it is not me.

"On a night like this one. In a place like this right here." I pointed to the dense forest surrounding the car. "There was a little boy who went to bed and heard a scratching on the window."

"This is not a scary story."

"I'm not done." I glanced at my wife in the passenger seat and continued. "Anyway, this little boy began to wonder what was scratching the window, so he went to look. And there just outside his window was the Nut-boy."

"Dad...what...is...a...Nut-boy?" Emma asked, her breathy voice chopping like a computer voice program from the 1990s.

"I'm glad you asked, Emma. The Nut-boy was a boy from an area near here who would sneak into bedrooms at night and eat the fingers and toes of little kids."

Now I don't know about any of you, but a boy sneaking into my childhood bedroom and eating my fingers or toes would have terrified me as a child.

"That's not scary," said the five-year-old Emma critic behind me.

I took the evaluation as a challenge. "You know the Nut-boy was spotted near here just last week. He was hiding near the road and throwing rocks at passing cars to knock out the engines. He would then break into the cars and eat the children's fingers and toes." I took the car out of gear and pressed on the gas pedal revving the engine. I glanced at my wife. She did not look entirely pleased, but she did not demand that I stop. "What happened? The engine isn't working."

"Dad...did...the...Nut-boy...hit...the...engine...with...a ...rock?"

"I don't know, Emma. I will pull over and see what happened."

"Dad, you're lying," Dylan chuckled, but there was a hint of worry as his right thumb darted into his mouth, and his left hand began pulling on his left ear.

The car drifted off to the side of the road onto the narrow shoulder slowly coming to a stop near a large group of cedar trees. I revved the engine for effect, and then looked over my shoulder at my children locked in their child seats. "I think I saw something in the woods. I think I saw something move behind the car. I'm going to roll the windows down so you guys can see." As soon as the windows began moving both children screamed loudly.

"Roll up the windows," my wife intervened. She looked at me like I was a junior high boy who had just farted in her class. I rolled up the windows, put the car in gear and pulled back onto the road, pleased that I managed to scare my children.

"That wasn't scary," Dylan said.

Before I could respond my wife verbally stepped between the two immature males in the car, one six-year-old and one thirty-eight-year-old. "We are done with scary stories tonight," she announced.

That night the kids snuck into our room and slept in our bed.

A week later after a day in Olympia we were heading home through the dark. "Dad...tell...us...a...scary...story," Emma requested.

"I'm not going to tell you guys a story because you can't handle it," I replied.

"I wasn't scared."

"I...wasn't...scared."

"Why did you end up sleeping in my bed then?"

"Tell us a story. We won't sleep in your bed."

It was a beautiful Western Washington coastal evening. A full moon shown over the tidal flats and wetlands giving all the cedar and spruce trees a yellowish glow. The afternoon fog and breeze had evaporated into clear skies and mild temperatures. It was the perfect evening for a scary story.

As I mulled over the possible story ideas a thought entered my mind: what if I drove down by the John's River boat launch and got out of the car? Now that would be scary.

John's River came twisting out of a dense evergreen forest and meandered through about three hundred acres of wetlands before running by a boat launch near John's River Bridge and out into the mouth of Grays Harbor. Under the full moon, the shadows of the trees, the slow-moving water, the bridge, the wetlands would all provide an especially creepy environment to end my story-telling that evening.

Ten miles from the boat launch is the Stafford Creek Correctional Facility, rural America's greatest growing industry: a prison. As we passed the correctional facility I started my story, "Did you hear the Nut-boy escaped from this prison right here? He escaped on a night just like this one. He wandered into the woods and waited. He was waiting for some new victims, some young victims, some young victims with plump fingers and toes."

"This isn't scary," Dylan laughed.

"Dad...is...the...Nut-boy...real?"

"Sure Emma, the Nut-boy is real."

"No, he isn't Emma. Your Father is telling a scary story," my wife cut in. "The Nut-boy is just a story."

"Dad is just trying to scare us Emma." Dylan laughed again.

"Oh...this...isn't...scary." Emma laughed along with her brother.

"Did you see that?" I asked, "I just saw the Nut-boy standing by the edge of the road." The laughter stopped, and I could hear Dylan sucking on his thumb.

As the road emerged from the forest and headed out across the open wetlands towards John's River, I shouted, "There he is! I see him! Do you see him running across the wetlands? I see him. Let's go get him!"

"No...Dad."

Dylan pulled his thumb out of his mouth long enough to assure his sister, "He's joking. There isn't any Nut-boy. This isn't scary anyway."

"This isn't a story, Dylan, this is real. I see him down there by John's River. It looks like he is going to swim across. Let's catch him. I'm going to catch him!" I slowed down as we drove over the bridge, and then I turned on the turn signal.

"Jon, where are you taking us?" my wife whispered.

"Just down to the boat launch," I said as quietly as I could. We pulled off the main road and turned onto the dirt road leading down to the boat launch. The wheels rolling over the gravel crackled, and the sucking noise from the backseat increased. "Keep your eyes open kids, and let me know if you see him." There was no response. This would have been a great place to end the story, a mature adult would have ended the story here, but you already know all about my maturity level. Instead I pulled the car down to the water's edge, close enough to make my wife tense her body. "Look around kids, do you see him?"

No response. Dylan sucked on his thumb so loudly it sounded like we had a baby calf in the backseat.

I glanced into the rearview mirror, "I see him! He's behind the car!"

"Run him over!" Dylan blurted.

"I'll get him!" I opened my door and both of my tiny, innocent children screamed. Leaving the door open, I hopped out of the car and ran toward the trunk. I knew neither of the kids could see me since they were locked down in their car seats, so I let the evening take over for a moment. I stood behind the car listening to the pleas of my children before I scrunched down low and snuck up beside Dylan's window and like the mature adult I am, sprung up into his field of vision, screaming like a madman. The look of terror on his face is not something I am proud of, but like any storyteller, I was happy I managed to pull off a successful scary story.

I stood up, walked around the car and got into the driver's seat. Both of the children were quiet, but as soon as I pulled the car out of the dirt road and back onto the pavement Dylan said, "That wasn't scary."

"My ears are still ringing from your screams."

"It wasn't scary."

"Dylan, you were scared," my wife said with a laugh.

"I...was...scared...dad."

"Were you Emma? I thought that would be a good scary story."

Both kids spent the night sleeping in our bed.

The "scary story" became a tradition of late-night drives, and I expanded my repertoire while toning down the theatrics.

There was a giant banana slug that slithered out of the fog and pressed itself up against doors, waiting for someone to get the morning paper. The police would find a long slick trail of ooze leading off into the ocean. The giant slug eventually met its match when our dog Steffi sniffed it out and alerted the authorities. All the stories from that point became opportunities for "Steffi the Wonderdog" to rescue the family.

Next was the armless crab fisherman who wandered the beach dunes crying out, "I wants me arms. Who has me arms?" I did not think that this story was especially scary, but Emma actually told me to stop telling it.

"Dad...I'm...scared...stop."

"Emma he's an armless fisherman. He can't even open a door." That information helped some but until "Steffi the Wonderdog" attacked the fisherman the kids were eerily quiet.

Then there were the little people who snuck into houses and stole things that weren't put away. These little people seemed unthreatening to me, but once we got home the kids picked up all their toys. Dylan told me years later that he would get up in the middle of the night and check to see if the little people were there.

My children remember every detail of each story and spent nights in their rooms fearful of the various monsters running through their minds. Emma refused to go out to the hot tub if it was foggy. "What...about...the...giant...slug?"

I remembered being terrified of many things as a child, and my parents did not tell me scary stories. My Dad did tell me one time that the meat in beef stroganoff was made from cowboy fingers; I never ate beef stroganoff again. The flying monkeys in the *Wizard of Oz* gave me nightmares. The child catcher in *Chitty Chitty Bang Bang* sent me scurrying for safety every time I watched the movie. There were people in my neighborhood who scared me, people in wheelchairs scared me, trees scared me, thunder scared me, shadows, old people, gopher holes and heights all scared me. I spent a good portion of my childhood cowering in a corner.

I wondered about what it must be like for my children growing up in a house where the father, the protector, was busy doing everything he could to terrify his children. I looked at the wild land surrounding our home with a child's eye instead of an adult one. There were terrifying dark places surrounding our house enclosed by overgrown bushes and trees just feet from our home. Along our driveway was an abandoned house that was slowly caving in upon itself. The front door was gone, the windows had all been smashed, and the brick chimney leaned like the tower in Pisa. The house was so scary in the daylight that I had only looked in through the windows and never ventured beyond the threshold of the front door. At night I had a feeling that rats and other furry rodents battled it out on the floors and walls of the structure. I could only imagine what kinds of terrors a place like that would hold in a child's mind.

I decided that it was time to stop telling scary stories. It was time to grow up and begin nurturing my children. It was a good, mature decision, a decision that lasted about two weeks.

One evening we were heading home from Olympia. My mother-in-law happened to be along with us and as we cruised toward Westport, Dylan requested a scary story.

"I'm not telling you guys scary stories anymore because you can't handle it."

"Your stories don't scare us. We won't get scared."

"Dad...tell...us...a...story. A...scary...story."

I continued on the adult high road deflecting the insults for about ten minutes. "Okay, I will tell you a very short scary story." My plan was to stall until we got home and then say, "Boo." It would make my wife happy, my mother-in-law would think that her daughter had married an adult, and I would look like the mature man I kind of wanted to be.

So, I continued leading the kids on until we arrived at our driveway. As I turned onto the dirt road Dylan said, "I knew you couldn't scare us. I knew you weren't going to tell us a scary story."

We were about one hundred yards from our house, and I should have been able to make it, but the juvenile delinquent in me took over. I began rolling everyone's windows down and turned off the headlights. I cut the engine and rolled the car right next to the abandoned house. That was it: windows down, lights off, parked next to the most terrifying house within twenty miles.

I am certain that the neighbors living hundreds of feet away on all sides heard my children screaming; some of the neighbors might have even considered calling 911, but after five seconds of screams I rolled the windows back up, turned the car on and drove into our carport. Once the car had come to a complete stop I turned to the kids. "Pretty scary huh?"

My mother-in-law looked a bit shell-shocked and none too pleased.

Dylan shot back, "I wasn't scared."

That night the kids crawled into our bed and slept secure in the knowledge that I was still one of them.

The Land Baron

Carl wanted to own land, so when he saw the ad in the *Sequim Gazette,* he called the number. "I'm calling about the land you advertised."

"Land? I think you have the wrong number. I have two cemetery plots I want to sell, but I don't have any land for sale."

"No, yeah that's the land I wanted to buy."

"The cemetery plots?"

"Yeah, the cemetery land. It says here, 'Two choice plots overlooking ocean. Need to sell. $1400 obo.' That's you, right?"

"Yes, that's my ad. Did you want to buy the plots?"

"Can I take a look at them first?"

"Sure, do you want to meet at the cemetery?"

"Yes, I would like to look at the land before I buy."

"Okay, let's meet at 6:30 tomorrow evening after I get off work, so you can look at the land."

"Right by the entrance?"

"Huh?"

"Do you want to meet by the entrance?"

"Oh, sure, let's meet by the entrance."

Carl hardly slept that night. The following day at work Carl told everyone he was going to buy some land. Grace, who worked with Carl most of the day, wondered how a 25-year-old Safeway bagboy was going to buy land in Port Angeles with an ocean view and free lawn maintenance, but she wasn't curious enough to ask. Carl was a talker, and sometimes his stories didn't always reflect reality, at least, everyone else's reality.

After work, Carl drove his mom's Cadillac to Walmart and bought a lawn chair. He opened and sat in each chair, a modern-day Goldilocks in the narrow aisles, until he found the one that was just right: a blue beach chair with a drink holder in the armrest. Carl folded up the chair, waited five minutes in a line of three people to purchase it, and then tossed it in the trunk of the car. He made a quick stop by the bank and withdrew $1000 cash and then it was off to the Ocean View Cemetery.

As Carl pulled up the hillside toward the cemetery, a panorama opened to the north. White waves crashed into the craggy coastline far below, so far below he could not hear the water tearing away at the land. The blue Pacific, the yellow sky, the cool evening breeze and the soaring birds were too much for Carl, and his eyes filled with tears.

Standing at the gate was a man in a black suit leaning against a black BMW. The man was younger than Carl had imagined, much younger. Carl pulled the car up beside the man and rolled down the window. "Are you the guy selling the land?"

"Yeah, I'm the guy selling the land. Follow me. I'll take you to the land." He gave the second "land" a sarcastic twist that Carl didn't like.

Carl rolled up his window, gave the BMW space to pass and followed. The two cars snaked through the Ocean View Cemetery until they reached a slight rise in the hillside. The BMW stopped and Carl parked behind. The man in the black suit got out of the car, admired himself in the black reflection, and buttoned his suit jacket. "The plots are over here," he said moving toward a large pine tree.

Carl popped open his trunk, took out his beach chair, and followed the man to the plots.

"Here they are." The man noticed the folding chair. "Going to stay awhile?"

"Just wanted to get a feel for the spot," Carl said unfolding the chair and setting it in the middle of the two marked plots. The view was everything Carl had hoped for. The pine tree gave just enough shade to keep the grass green and allowed just enough light to keep the moss down. The view of the Pacific was unimpeded.

"Well, what do you think? Do you want to buy them?"

"I am interested. The ad said $1,400 or best offer right?"

"Yeah, actually I had a guy offer me $1,750 right after you called, but I told him you had first dibs." The man had misjudged Carl. Carl was no sucker. Carl knew "or best offer" in an ad meant "desperate to sell," and Carl had already noticed the license plate holder on the BMW that read, "Bellevue BMW: Lease From Us." Carl also noticed the man's black suit looked good from a distance but was worn and slightly gray at the elbows up close.

Carl hiked up his pants and shifted into his garage sale tone. "I brought $1,000 cash."

"Sure, you could pay me $1,000 now and 750 later. That would work."

"No, I'll pay you $1,000 now, and that's it."

"Okay, I guess I'll sell the plots to the other guy. You're passing up a great deal here."

Carl could hear the anxiety in the man's voice. "All right," Carl stood up and folded his chair and began walking back to the Cadillac.

"Wait, wait a minute. I don't know why I am doing this."

Carl knew why.

After work each day Carl visited his land. He set up his chair, put a drink in the armrest, and sat down to enjoy the view. The cemetery workers left around five, so Carl's presence went unnoticed. People visiting deceased loved ones did not notice Carl either. He enjoyed his insignificance.

On days when the weather was not ideal, Carl brought along his father's old golf umbrella and wrapped himself tightly in a fleece blanket. He would fill a thermos with hot chocolate and watch the waves beat against the rocks below. The white foam churning and fighting the currents had a beauty Carl appreciated. He himself felt tossed uncontrollably by the forces of nature. His parents left him with the things of life: car, house, lawn mower, washer/dryer. But he felt unequipped to meet the shifts of living in the world today. His land gave him the sense of peace his parents left him without, which was funny because his parents were both buried less than 200 yards from his land.

He never visited their gravesites.

One evening after work Carl pulled into the Ocean View Cemetery to find it full of cars and people. Carl considered going home and coming back tomorrow, but he figured he could blend in with the crowd, and then they would all go home.

He drove slowly to his land, twisting in and out between the parked cars and found his spot. He set up his chair, wrapped himself in his blanket, and poured himself a cup of hot chocolate.

It was a large funeral; Carl guessed 1,500 people were there. He wondered who would be so important that 1,500 people would show up to their funeral. Carl would have to wait for a few weeks before he would know who died because the headstones took some time to be placed.

The service looked to be a traditional affair from where Carl sat. Some praying, some speaking, some crying, and then everyone began leaving. Once everyone was gone two cemetery workers came out of the shop area driving a tractor that pulled a flat trailer. The workers picked up chairs, rolled up AstroTurf, and eventually got to the work of interring the deceased. Carl watched with a great deal of interest as the workers lowered the casket and then picked up the silver platform the casket had been sitting on and set it on the trailer. One worker drove the platform into the shop and the other man began rolling up the AstroTurf that covered the sides of the grave and the mound of dirt. The tractor pulled back out of the shop with a different trailer this time. The trailer looked to Carl like one of those huge portable barbeque pits locals used for those salmon feeds to fundraise money for the Elks, but instead of a hanging grill surface, there was a large rectangular cement lid swinging from the contraption. The worker skillfully pulled the trailer around the grave and backed it over the hole.

As the worker got off of the tractor, he pointed in Carl's direction. Then both men turned and looked at Carl. Carl waved. The workers paused a second and waved back. They went back to work lowering the cement lid into the hole, and then the driver took the tractor back into the shop. When he came walking back out, there was a bald man with him. As they walked the worker pointed in Carl's direction, and the bald man looked directly at Carl.

Carl waved.

The bald man did not wave back.

The bald man did not stop at the gravesite; he kept walking, walking directly to Carl's land.

"Are you here for the funeral?" The bald man asked breathing heavily.

"No," Carl said without going any further.

"No?"

"Nope."

"Then do you mind if I ask why you are here looking like you are watching a football game?"

"No," Carl said with a hardness that surprised the bald man.

"No, you don't mind?" The bald man's voice strained.

"No, I don't mind. You can ask."

"Why are you here?" The bald man paused after each word pointing to the ground.

"I'm visiting my land."

"Your land?"

"Yes, my land. This is my land," Carl said pointing to the ground.

"This is not your land. This land belongs to the Port Angeles Cemetery."

"You mean the Ocean View Cemetery?"

"Yeah, whatever. You can't stay here."

"I own this land, I have the paperwork, and I am not leaving."

"You own this land? You mean you own these plots? Owning the land and owning the plots are two different things."

"I can show you the paperwork."

"I don't want to see the paperwork. I want you to leave before I have to call the police."

"Start dialing. It's my land, and I'm not leaving."

"You're going to be sorry," the bald man said as he turned and stomped back to the shop office.

Two days later Carl's name appeared in the local law and order section of the *Peninsula Daily News*: trespassing and resisting arrest.

On Tuesday, Susan Johnson, a reporter for the *PDN*, overheard the Sheriff talking about Carl's arrest.

Locals gathered at the Chestnut Cottage Restaurant for morning coffee, pancakes, and gossip. Susan came every morning hoping for moments just like this one: Sheriff Hanson role-playing an arrest for the two other deputies at his table.

"So I get there and say, 'Okay, Carl, it's time to go,' and he says, 'It's my land and I ain't moving' so I say it one more time, and this time I put my hand on my peacemaker like this." The Sheriff moved his right hand to his side with his elbow out.

"Is this Carl Pense? The kid whose parents died in that swimming accident a few years ago?" the taller deputy asked.

"Suicide you mean," the Sheriff said.

"You think it was a suicide?" the fat deputy cut in.

"Of course it was a suicide, Mills. Who goes swimming in the ocean in November, two days after they update their wills and life insurance? Couldn't prove it though. Pretty slick if you think about it.

"Anyway, I says to Carl, 'Let's go. Time to go Carl' and the little bastard says, 'You gonna shoot me?' and I says, 'Well, we wouldn't have to move you far afterwards.'" The sheriff paused allowing the deputies' laughter to die. "So I reach around and get my cuffs and say, 'Carl you are under arrest,' and the bastard doesn't move. He just sits there wrapped up in his blanket like a baby and pulls his arms in tighter like this."

Susan Johnson had her notepad out and was jotting down details.

"So I move in for the kill. I got my cuffs in one hand, and I can't grab his arm because he's all wrapped up in this damn blanket. He just kinda worms around in his chair, and I try to grab him until I slip and come falling down on him, just smashing his beach chair and landing right on top of him. I think I knocked the wind out of 'em."

"I'll bet," the tall deputy laughed.

"Is that a fat joke, Wallace?"

"No sir, no sir. I just meant with his arms all tucked in he couldn't probably keep you from landing on him."

"Yeah, sure." The Sheriff gave Wallace a cold look. "So anyway, we start rolling around right there on *his land*. He starts yelling, 'This is my land. You can't do this.' And then he starts bawling. I wasn't sure if he was bawling 'cause he was hurt or if he was just being a baby."

"Just being a baby," Mills said shaking his head.

"It was his chair. He was crying because I broke his chair. He's like, 'You broke my chair. You broke my chair.' I damn near died laughing. But he went to wipe his tears with his hand, and I grabbed his damn arm and nearly twisted it off. Then he starts crying about being hurt. 'You're hurtin' my arm. You're hurtin' my arm.' So I get him twisted around face down and cuff him and shove him in the back of the cruiser. When it was all over, I looked like I had been in a real to-do. My shirt was all untucked, hair was a mess, and I had grass stains all over my pants. I could just imagine what the little woman was going to say when she saw my uniform."

Susan Johnson had heard enough; she paid the waitress and went to the office.

Susan Johnson's article, "A Fight For Land" took up half the front page of the *Peninsula Daily News* the next day. A 4"x4" picture of Carl Pense holding his broken beach chair was placed strategically on the fold enticing the readers to open the paper to see the whole story. The editor selected a pullout quote from Carl to jump out at the casual reader. "People never get to enjoy their cemetery plots. I just wanted to enjoy mine."

Susan investigated the incident, interviewed all of the parties involved and wrote a tight and interesting article. "Dog bites man is not news, but man bites dog is," Susan remembered her Journalism professor saying, and she had stumbled upon a man biting a dog. It was not her first front-page article, but it was the first article the AP wires picked up and sent around the globe. They knew a good man-bites-dog article when they saw one.

The website at the *PDN* became a flurry of traffic. The comment pages filled with conflicting views on Carl's actions from all over the world. Carl was both hero and scoundrel.

Then Carl's phone began ringing. It kept ringing and ringing. At first Carl was happy to answer the questions from reporters around the world and country, but how many times can a person answer the same five questions? Carl had not signed up to become a beacon of goodness or evil amidst the confusion of the world. Carl unplugged his phone. He wanted to sit on his land and watch the white foam churn. Then the letters began arriving, bags and bags of letters. Carl opened each letter and kept the good ones.

At work people now noticed him. Kids took pictures of him for their Facebook pages, old ladies requested Carl's assistance loading their groceries, and skateboarders told him he was their hero. Carl's life had shifted from human existence to icon.

Walmart's narrow outdoor furniture aisles became crowded with elderly people looking for the perfect chair. Never before had Walmart sold so much outdoor furniture so late in the year. The store manager was baffled, but his regional manager said that the lawn furniture was "selling like hotcakes" all over the United States.

Mysterious newspapers began appearing in Carl's mailbox. *The Tribune* from San Luis Obispo arrived first. On the front page was a large 4"x 6" picture, centered on the fold, of hundreds of elderly men and women sitting on lawn chairs at the local cemetery. The pullout quote from Emma Oxenrider said, "That young man was right. We don't get to enjoy our plots."

Carl clipped the articles and put them on his refrigerator, and when there was no more room on his fridge, he put them in an old picture album.

After a few weeks, the trespassing and resisting arrest charges against Carl were quietly dismissed. How could they prosecute Carl when the cemetery was now filled with living people sitting on lawn chairs each evening?

A month after the incident the Sheriff pulled his cruiser into Carl's driveway. Carl felt his gut tighten as he watched the Sheriff get out of the car, open the trunk, and pull out a large rectangular box. Carl came out of the house before the Sheriff got to the porch. "What do you want?" Carl asked.

"Carl, I'm sorry about what happened, but you didn't leave me many options."

"What's in the box? You got something in there that you're going to hit me with?"

"No, Carl, I made you this," the Sheriff said pulling a beautiful wooden chair out of the box. The Sheriff's reputation as a woodworker was well known in the town, and he often sold expensive handmade furniture at the local farmers' market. "I tried to make it light, so you can get it in and out of your trunk, and I put this hinge here, so it will fold up nearly flat. I wanted to see how it fit you."

Carl took the chair and unfolded it and set it on his porch.

"I made it an Adirondack style because I thought it would be the most comfortable."

Carl sat in the chair. It fit. The wood was smooth from hours of fine sanding and Carl melted into the seat.

"You can take it up to Ocean View any time you want. There won't be any more trouble," the Sheriff said. "You'll have lots of company up there."

Carl let his bitterness leave. "Thanks, Sheriff."

Carl spent the next thirty-five years enjoying his land. His will specified, "Sprinkle me on my land. I don't want to be buried."

The Hood Canal Bridge

One day, while driving across that illogical strip of cement,
Neptune asked, "How can concrete float?"
I did not know.
The worlds of Mythology and Engineering are beyond me.
I live in the world of words, where all things are possible.

A world where churning flames of water boil
And shatter against floating stone.
A world where 30 feet away from chaos
the waters are so pure Narcissus could lean
over the cold rail and be entranced.

I do not question these worlds,
like the churning waters, they are in me.
The façade between inward
and outward does not matter.
Deep below the chaos and calm mix.

Is it Myth?
It is Science?
Or, is it the magic of worlds, laid bit by bit
across two wild chunks of land
connecting things never intended to connect.

Christmas with Dad

One day, sometime in late December, I came home from school to find out my father had cut off the tip of his finger. Apparently, he was rushing to finish a woodworking project for Christmas and in his haste forgot where his fingers ended and where the board started. Fortunately for my father, he was not a concert pianist or a sign-language translator. His job as a Presbyterian Pastor could be done with ten fingers or nine and a half.

For the next four years my father spent each Christmas service damaged in some way. It was tradition for our family: December arrives, Dad injures himself, Dad has a big bandage covering one of his extremities, Christmas arrives.

The tip of the finger was never located, and whenever I swept the garage I feared moving boxes or looking into dark corners, because I knew somewhere in that garage was a bit of my father that had been displaced. I even wondered if the fingertip might have jumped into one of the drawers of my bed. It didn't help that there was a movie out at the time called *The Hand* where a disembodied hand crawled around looking for revenge. I knew one day I would find something in the garage that looked like a large raisin, and upon further investigation I would discover it was a chunk of my Dad.

That Christmas my Dad addressed the congregation with a large bandage wrapped around his right index finger: the beginning of a tradition.

The next year it was my father's back. He was lifting something in the garage when his back went out. Many years before, he had injured his back playing basketball when someone undercut him; he flipped and landed on his tailbone. It was an injury that would crop up occasionally, and this time it immobilized him immediately.

He crumpled to the ground and could not move. This usually wouldn't be a problem, but because all the kids were at school and mom was at work, he had to lie on the floor until he could move. He tried to stand but couldn't. He tried to crawl on all fours and couldn't. Finally, he dragged himself into the house and over to the phone. The phone was hanging on the wall, so he had to pull it off the hook by shaking the cord. Evidently this whole process took close to two hours. He finally called our youth director who came and plopped him on a flat couch. My Dad built this orange-colored 1970s couch in the garage. The four of us kids could fit on it and watch the television for one hour a day with only four channels.

When I got home, there he was, all 6'4" of him, flat on his back. He would remain there until after Christmas which, as I recall, was still a week away. He had his meals lying flat, he watched television lying flat, and he even had a special bottle and bedpan. Dad became part of the Christmas décor. There was the tree, there were the stockings, there was the manger, and there was Dad tucked neatly under some festive covers near the presents.

Even though the entire Christmas season was a bit strange it was the most memorable and special Christmas I recall. One night I was Dad's nurse. I took care of the man who had taken care of me for so many years. During the evening he asked for my help in surprising the family. He had stashed a new color television in one of our neighbor's houses and needed me to get it on Christmas Eve. I felt privileged to fill my father's role as the Christmas surprise guy and looked forward to sneaking across the street to retrieve the new TV set.

The most important Christmas tradition was the Christmas Eve candlelight service. This was a special ceremony because at the end of the service I got to drip hot wax from a candle all over my hand without getting in trouble. My father would always spend a great deal of time on the service, and I usually enjoyed the ceremony, but since it was Christmas Eve time seemed to stand still.

The year my Dad threw out his back, he was unable to lead the service; in fact he was at home lying flat as Kansas listening to the service on the phone. I sat in the back of the church holding up the phone so he could hear how it was going. One of the church elders led the procedure and did a fair job. Dad had written out the message and planned the entire service just like he was Shakespeare.

My arm got tired a few times, but I knew how important it was for my dad to hear the whole thing, so I fought through the discomfort and held up the receiver throughout. As the ceremony came to an end and the candles were being passed around, I put the receiver to my ear and told my dad that I was going to hang up now. On the other end, I could hear him snoring. I don't know at what point he started snoozing, but it is safe to say that he is probably the only minister in the history of the world to ever have his own sermon put him to sleep.

When Christmas Day finally arrived, we gathered around the tree and opened our presents as family tradition dictated, one at a time. Dad lay in the middle of the mess and smiled the entire day, at least until we opened the last present, then Dad started to cry. I hadn't seen my Dad cry before and so none of the kids knew what to do. Dad blubbered something about how everyone had been so good to him and how happy he was; hearing my Dad say those things was the first time I enjoyed Christmas more for the event than the stuff I got. We all gave each other hugs and felt good about being in *this* family for the first time in a long time.

Dad kept up his end of the bargain as far as tradition went. For some reason Dad had a strong dislike for the stray cat my older sister had brought home, and he never seemed to warm to the idea of having a cat in the house. This cat was constantly sharpening its claws on the furniture and carpet and since Dad worked to pay for those things the cat was doomed to end up "disappearing" one day.

Maybe the cat sensed my father's dislike and did just enough to annoy him without causing its own demise, but about a week before Christmas the cat stepped over the line. Dad came into the living room to find the cat scratching away on the couch. Dad yelled at the cat and was soon chasing this tiny feline around the house, until it made a break for the upstairs. Dad's chasing days came to an abrupt end as he smashed his big toe into one of the stairs breaking his foot.

The cat escaped to torment my father another day, and Dad was left hopping around the house until Mom could run him to the hospital.

Dad came home in a large walking cast.

That Christmas Dad hobbled around the church and delivered his sermon looking something like an oversized version of what I imagined Tiny Tim looked like from *A Christmas Carol*.

People in the congregation started to tease my Dad about his yearly injuries. He was good-natured about the whole thing, but I wonder if he started to dread December.

The next year Dad was back to his old tricks.

The house we had moved into the year before was an older structure, and one of the oddities was that the electrical outlets were on the floor and not on the wall. This didn't particularly interest me until one day, right around Christmas, the cat decided to pee on one of the outlets. I am sure the cat got a little surprise but managed to escape without permanent damage. My Dad was not so lucky.

The cat's pee hit the outlet and caused some kind of electrical spark to shoot out. The spark hit a curtain hanging just above the outlet, catching it on fire. The flame was already near the ceiling when Superdad appeared to save the day. He grabbed the curtain and pulled it off its hanger and threw it on the ground where he stomped the fire out. Regrettably, the curtain was made of some nylon-like fabric that melted all over my Dad's hand and arm, burning him severely. He didn't seem to notice at first, I think he wanted to find the cat and see if her fur was fireproof, but soon his burnt arm signaled his brain that he was about to take his yearly trip to the ER.

So that Christmas, Dad stood in front of his congregation looking quite normal. His right arm was completely covered with white gauze from his fingertips to his elbow. He delivered his sermon, never mentioning his injury and led the candle lighting ceremony. The next day it was Christmas. We opened presents one at a time, and Dad stood amidst the mess bandaged to the hilt. He smiled throughout the unwrapping of presents and was probably wondering what would happen next year, but the next year came and went without incident, and then another year came and went and another and another.

Two years ago we went to have Christmas with Mom and Dad. My kids were very excited as we pulled up into Grandma and Grandpa's driveway. They hopped out of the car and sprinted into the house looking for their grandparents, but the house was empty. My wife and I looked around and called out for my parents, but no one was home. I went into the kitchen and found a loaf of sourdough bread half cut; nearby was a sharp knife and a trickle of blood on the floor leading out the door. Instinctively, I called the local hospital and asked if they had someone named Eekhoff there.

They did. A Christmas tradition was reborn.

Little Jesus

Peter came to his first day of second grade in a purple robe. Most kids arrived with parents, but not Peter; he walked into the class, found his desk, and sat without saying a word.

Mrs. Sanders wasn't sure what to do. The first day was difficult for students, a new class, a new teacher, a new group of friends, and a new way of doing things. Most second graders squirmed in their desks waiting for Mrs. Sanders to start class; Peter sat gazing at the ceiling, his right hand near his chin, index and forefinger raised as if he were preparing to bless someone.

"Good morning, children. My name is Mrs. Sanders. Can you say, 'Good morning, Mrs. Sanders,' when I say good morning to you? Let's try that. Good morning, children."

"Good morning, Mrs. Sanders," the class shouted.

"Well, aren't you all full of energy? Did you all have a good summer? I sure did, but I could not wait to start school this year, because I knew you would be here."

Peter raised his hand. Mrs. Sanders hesitated. "Yes?"

Peter stood next to his desk before speaking. "Mrs. Sanders, someone has touched my robe."

The class was quiet. The squirming stopped. "Someone

has touched your robe?"

"Yes. Someone has touched my robe, and because of their faith I will heal them."

"Oh," Mrs. Sanders paused, "we should all be respectful of each other's things, and we shouldn't touch others unless it's okay."

"I would like to heal the child who has touched my robe."

Mrs. Sanders smiled, "Well, Peter, this is a public school. We will have to save the healing for recess."

"Okay," Peter turned to the class, "Whoever touched my robe, come see me at recess and I will heal you." He sat back down, retook his pose gazing off into the distance.

Mrs. Sanders moved on, but noticed half of the class was not listening; they stared toward the ceiling to see what Peter saw. "Children. Children. I need your eyes up here. Let's take out a pencil and paper and prepare to write about your summer."

The class complied, and Mrs. Sanders drifted around to see what the children were writing. Then she came to Peter's desk. Colored pencils were spread out across his desktop, and there, on his paper, was a large red, illuminated M. The detail stopped Mrs. Sander's breath. Little blue birds flew around the giant M, and thick brown ivy branches spread out around the page diminishing into small vines as they moved away from the letter. Peter was highlighting the bottoms of the ivy leaves with a dark green pencil when Mrs. Sanders stopped and bent down, "Did you just do this?"

"Yes, my child," Peter said without looking up.

"My goodness, Peter. It is lovely."

"Bless you," he said turning his face toward her. From a distance, Peter appeared to be just another grubby second grader who's face needed a good scrubbing, but now Mrs. Sanders could see someone had scribbled a brown mustache and beard on his face in eye liner pencil. "Can I finish this tonight?"

"Certainly, Peter. It's beautiful. You take as much time as you need, sweet pea." Peter turned his face back to the page and continued. Mrs. Sanders walked around the room looking at each child's paper feeling let down: crooked letters, sloppy writing, misspellings, and Appalachian grammar.

At recess, Mrs. Sanders watched Peter from behind her classroom window. He did not climb the monkey bars, he did not swing on the swings, and he was not interested in playing games. He strolled, left hand holding his robe so it didn't drag on the ground, right hand in the air making the sign of the cross. Peter's lips flexed and protruded in bold movements as if he were speaking to a large group. Mrs. Sanders held her breath.

Peter wandered the playground for another minute and then approached a boy. Mrs. Saunders's jaw tightened. The two boys talked, Peter gestured, touched the boy on the forehead, and continued his walk. The second boy followed. Within ten minutes Peter had talked to, blessed, and assembled a dozen boys into his flock, all of them trailing Peter toward the swings.

Grace Schrader was swinging high into the morning air when Peter approached. Peter motioned. His followers grabbed the chains of Grace's swing, stopping her with a jolt. Mrs. Sanders's heart raced. She could not see what was happening, but ten seconds later Peter finished his business with Grace. The bell rang and the crowds headed back to their classrooms.

As the children filed in Mrs. Sanders waited for Grace, "Grace, may I speak with you a moment? The rest of you go into class, sit down, and wait." Mrs. Sanders waited a moment, "Grace, what happened? Grace, where are your glasses?"

"Peter healed my eyes. I don't need them anymore."

"What?" Mrs. Sanders bent down next to Grace. "Peter did what?"

"He healed my eyes. I touched his robe, and he healed my eyes. He rubbed mud on my eyes, and now I can see."

"He did what?"

"He got some dirt, spit in it, and rubbed it on my eyes. Now I can see without my glasses."

Mrs. Sanders looked at Grace's eyelids; she could see where Peter's grubby little fingers left their muddy mark. "Okay, go in and sit down."

Mrs. Sanders spent most of "Math Time" worrying. She could not quiet her inner voice. She wasn't sure how, but somehow all of this would fall on her. She would be asked why she didn't do something about the little boy who had gone mad in her class. She tried to teach math, but her heart wasn't in it; she wanted a cigarette, three shots of Crown Royal, and a pint of Ben and Jerry's.

The staff room was noisy when Mrs. Sanders arrived to eat lunch.

"Hey, Rhonda, one of my kids told me last period he became a disciple of one of your kids," Mr. Raymond blurted out before she had taken two steps into room. "Sounds like you've got a real live one on your hands this year."

"Yes, Peter Jones. Who had Peter Jones last year?" Mrs. Sanders asked as she moved toward the long table.

"Peter Jones?" Mrs. Miller said. "I had Peter last year. He was very quiet. What's he doing this year?"

Before Mrs. Sanders could answer, Mr. Raymond cut in. "He's dressed up like little Jesus walkin' around the playground converting disciples. I've got two in my class after last recess."

"Is that right, Rhonda?" Mrs. Miller asked.

"Yep, pretty much. He showed up this morning, all by himself, dressed like he was ready for Halloween. He healed Grace Schrader during first recess, and now she is insisting she doesn't need glasses."

"He healed Grace Schrader!" Mr. Raymond laughed, slapping the table. "I've got a few to send his way if he is healing kids."

"Well, good luck contacting Peter's mother," Mrs. Miller said. "She's a tough one to find. Phone's disconnected. No email. She didn't show up for a single conference. Does that sound right? Anybody know the family?"

None of the teachers responded. "Great," Mrs. Sanders said digging into her lunch bag. "Any advice?"

"Stay on his good side. I hear his father can be a real fire and brimstone kind of guy." Mr. Raymond laughed pointing at the ceiling.

Outside, on the playground, Peter's twelve disciples gathered around the arched monkey bars watching as he climbed to the top. The recess monitors, Mrs. Ware and Ms. Mendez, were mediating a dispute on the kickball field and did not notice the little boy dressed in a purple robe climbing to the top of the arch. What the monitors noticed was the silence. When the monitors turned back to the play area they saw what would be termed from that day forward "The

Sermon on the Monkey Bars." Little Peter Jones stood atop the arch; all of the Meadow Lane Elementary school students surrounded the little boy in the purple robe in a silent trance.

"This is weird," Ms. Mendez said to Mrs. Ware.

"Do you think we should have him come down?"

"And interrupt this? No way," Ms. Mendez said.

"I like the way you think, Ruth. Is he reciting the Bible?"

"Sounds like it. Weird."

"Yep, weird. Who is that kid?"

"Dunno. I'll tell you this; I like him. He can come preach here every recess."

Peter preached to the multitude in King James English. "Blessed are they that mourn: for they shall be comforted. Blessed are the meek: for they shall inherit the Earth. Blessed are they that do hunger and thirst after righteousness: for they shall be filled." He did not rush through the language like a student who memorized something for class, but he spoke in a practiced, perfect tone. He paused. He turned toward different groups. He raised his voice to a shout and shook his fist. He comforted and cajoled, and when the recess bell rang, the students did not move until Peter concluded with, "Be ye therefore perfect, even as your Father which is in heaven is perfect. Bless you my children."

As Peter climbed down from his perch the crowd parted and scattered as if nothing unusual had happened during the first lunch recess of the year. Peter returned to class, sat in his seat, and stared at the ceiling until a note came from the office. Mrs. Sanders bent down next to Peter and handed him the note, "Don't worry, sweetie, you're not in trouble. Someone just wants to talk to you."

Peter turned to Mrs. Sanders, looked her in the eyes. "I

knew one of you would betray me."

Peter was gone the rest of the day.

After school Mrs. Sanders added the number two to the timeline, she watered the plants, and went through the student paragraphs about what they did during the summer. A few of the students had gone to Disneyland, one had traveled to Dinosaur National Park, but most wrote about watching TV or playing video games. After finishing the papers Mrs. Sanders realized Peter's was not there. She got up, walked over to Peter's "workstation" and looked inside the belly of his desk. It was empty except for a single sheet of paper sitting in the back corner. Mrs. Sanders reached in, pulled out the paper, looked at it, and collapsed. She curled into a ball, sobbing. She held the paper away from her body as if trying to escape from it, but the illuminated letters and image pressed into her brain. Bright red text flowed across the page, surrounded by elaborate ivy, running around the corners of the page and ending in a small skull in the bottom right hand corner of the page. Five words burned into Mrs. Sanders: "My daddy died this summer." Filling the space on the page was a drawing of stick figure man hanging from a tree.

The next day Peter wore his purple robe. Four classmates arrived wearing robes. Before the morning bell rang, three more boys arrived looking for Peter. Peter took the boys to his cubbyhole, pulled out three light brown tunics, and handed them over. Mrs. Sanders watched the exchange as if it was a drug deal but did not intervene.

Peter's four classroom disciples spent the morning mimicking Peter's every move. If he stared into the corner, they stared into the corner; if he knotted his hands together, they knotted their hands; if he raised his hand, they raised their hands.

During recess Mrs. Sanders looked out the window and saw Peter strolling the grounds followed by twelve boys dressed in robes.

After recess, Mrs. Sanders had a magical session of teaching that happens about once a month for teachers of her skill. The students were attentive. They asked questions, and Mrs. Sanders had several "teachable moments." She talked about how math helped her with quilting and why it was always a bad idea to drink milk from the carton. As she walked the children to the lunchroom she felt good.

The staffroom was already as loud as the day before Christmas break, and the roar could be heard in the outer office. When Mrs. Sanders stepped through the door Mr. Raymond greeted her, shouting across the room, "Rhonda, did you know your little Jesus kid has kids in my class dressing in robes?"

"There are four of them in my class too," Mrs. Sanders said moving over to the refrigerator to get her lunch. "I saw him at recess walking around with all of his disciples following him."

"Yeah, I saw that, too. One kid from my class made a complete turnaround," Mr. Raymond said. "Yesterday this kid was one of those twitchy, can't sit still, ADHD squirmers who just can't stay in his seat. Today, it was like someone filled his water bottle with Ritalin. He sat there, asked questions, and didn't twitch at all. I'm ready to buy robes for my whole class if it keeps them quiet."

Mrs. Sanders sat down. "Yeah, I had one of my best teaching sessions ever before lunch, but I'm worried."

"About what?" Mrs. Miller asked.

"I'm not sure if I should say anything, but I gave a writing assignment yesterday about what the kids did over the summer."

"Same topic in my class." Mr. Raymond laughed.

"Well, most of the kids wrote about what they did, but Peter wrote 'My dad died' and then drew a picture of a man hanging from a tree." The lunchroom was silent.

"Rhonda, did you say your kid wrote his father died this summer?" Mr. Stein asked from the other end of the long table.

"Yes, he wrote his dad died over the summer and then drew a picture of a man hanging from a tree."

"Is the kid's last name Jones?" Mr. Stein asked.

"Yes, Peter Jones. Do you know the family?"

"I taught his father about twenty years ago. He was the Iraqi vet. PTSD. Hung himself this summer. It was all over the papers. I can't believe you weren't told. Rhonda, this kid needs to talk to someone," Mr. Stein said.

Mrs. Sanders closed her eyes, and bowed her head.

"It's okay, honey," Mrs. Miller said putting an arm around Mrs. Sanders. "It's going to be okay." The rest of the room was silent.

The door to the staff room shot open as the first tears rolled out of Mrs. Sanders' eyes. Mr. Watkins popped into the room laughing. "You guys will not believe what is going on in the cafeteria. I took a picture with my phone," he said presenting his iPhone to the closest staff member, "What's goin' on in here? Somebody run over a dog?"

Mr. Raymond looked at the iPhone screen. "Okay, I know the kid has problems, but this is hilarious. You guys have to look at this. Did they do this all by themselves?"

"Yeah, I turned around and there they all were lined up just like the painting."

"Take a look, Rhonda. This will cheer you up," Mr. Raymond said handing the phone toward Mrs. Sanders. Each teacher along the way looked at the phone and laughed.

"You didn't have them pose? I can't believe they ended up that way," said Mr. Raymond.

"Nope, I looked over and there they were. I don't know how they kept the one side of the table empty, or who brought the loaf of bread, but it is dead on, isn't it?"

The phone reached Mrs. Miller, who was now acting as Mrs. Sanders' protector. "Let me take a look." A small excited laugh escaped Mrs. Miller. "Oh my gosh. You must see this Rhonda." She held up the phone so Mrs. Sanders could see.

There on the tiny screen was a miniature version of DaVinci's *Last Supper*. Peter stood in the center of the screen, arms out toward the table as the two groups of disciples crowded together to his left and right. In the middle of the table was a loaf of bread broken in half. Mrs. Sanders pushed the phone away and got up from the table. She wanted to run. She wanted to go into the cafeteria, find Peter, pick him up and hold him. Instead she walked in a daze through the staff room door and left her colleagues.

The main office buzzed. Outside of Principal Parker's office door sat all twelve of the disciples. Mrs. Sanders approached Mrs. Hurst, the school secretary. "Why are they here?"

Mrs. Hurst signaled Mrs. Sanders to come close. "Wine. Your little fella brought wine to lunch. He passed around a big thermos of red wine to the whole group. He's in there right now with Bill. We can't get ahold of his mom, and he's not talkin'."

"Do you think it would be okay if I went in?"

"Let me call Bill and see." Mrs. Hurst picked up the phone, dialed Mr. Parker's extension and whispered, "Rhonda's out here, should she come in? Okay, okay. I'll tell her." She hung up. "He says not to go in right now. He's called CPS since the mom isn't pickin' up her phone. It sounds like your little fella is havin' a tough time, and Bill doesn't want him to get all upset again."

"Okay, should I wait, or just go back to my class?"

"Just go back, Rhonda. We'll handle it down here."

Mrs. Sanders wandered back to her room. She rolled the television cart to the front of the class and found the longest nature video in her collection. When her second graders returned from lunch recess the room was already dark. Mrs. Sanders said nothing. She turned on the television, pushed play, and the class watched two hours of *Planet Earth*. When the video was over Mrs. Sanders passed out paper and had the students draw pictures of their favorite animals until the final bell rang.

The next day Peter was not at school. Principal Parker told Mrs. Sanders that Peter had gone to a mental health facility. Mrs. Sanders taught her class. She said the words, she did the activities, but she spent her energy imagining Peter walking down white halls of a nondescript hospital, escorted by large men wearing white uniforms.

That night Mrs. Sanders dreamt of Peter. He had been placed in the mental ward with all the characters from *One Flew Over the Cuckoo's Nest*. Peter was not afraid. He remained calm even when Nurse Ratched screamed at him for wearing his purple robe. He walked the ward laying hands on the patients. He drove demons out of the sick men and made the lame whole again. Each action, each healing, angered Nurse Ratched, and she ordered him to stop touching other patients. When Peter refused, she locked him in a small, unlit, white room under her desk and left him there. He banged on the square door with his feet until he was exhausted, and then he wept. He promised to be a good boy and to never wear the robe again. Mrs. Sanders awoke and could not get back to sleep.

At five in the morning she gave up on sleeping and got up, got dressed and went to her classroom. She sat at her desk staring at Peter's workstation. She wanted it gone; she wanted to forget about the little boy in the purple robe. She stood up, walked to his desk, and lifted it. Something slid inside the desk. She set it back down and moved around to look inside the belly of the desk. Stuffed in the back was Peter's purple robe. It had not been there the day before. She pulled the robe from the desk and held it up to her nose. Her tears dappled the purple fabric, and she wept.

That night Mrs. Sanders dreamt Peter met Satan in the desert near Palm Springs. They stood on a bluff overlooking a collection of life-sized dinosaurs built in the 50s. Peter and Satan stood looking over the desert as the sun dropped toward the horizon.

"Let's walk down there, Peter," Satan said pointing toward the dinosaurs.

"Okay," Peter said. "I will walk with you, but you know I can't stay long."

"We have three days, Peter. You know that."

"Yes." Peter nodded, "Yes, I know."

As they walked side-by-side Satan tempted Peter with words, but Peter did not respond. Peter's robe dragged in the dirt and spiny plant seeds attached to the dusty cloth. Peter did not care. He let the robe gather all the dried, dead things without lifting the purple fabric from the ground.

"Peter, do you like dinosaurs?"

"I do. I like that one best," Peter said pointing at the Brontosaurus.

"Hmm. I like the T-Rex."

"You know *The Bible* says the meek shall inherit the Earth."

"I do know that. None of these animals inherited much."

"They're not animals. They're lizards."

"Peter, did you know you can climb inside the Brontosaurus?"

"No."

"Yes, you can climb up the neck to the mouth and see all the desert. Would you like to do that?"

"No, I don't like close places."

"You mean you fear small places? Places like closets?"

"Yes, closets scare me."

"Because of your father?"

"Yes."

"Peter, all of this could be yours," Satan said pointing to the dinosaurs standing in the desert.

"I don't want all of this," Peter said moving his arm from left to right.

"What do you want, Peter? I can give you whatever you want."

"Peter Jones," Mrs. Sanders found herself standing next to Peter. "Peter Jones, you will not make a deal with the devil."

Satan turned and glared at Mrs. Sanders. "I know you, Rhonda Sanders. You should not be giving advice to Peter Jones." His words slashed through Mrs. Sanders. "I know your heart, and I know what you don't want young Peter to know about you. So you be quiet."

Bile bubbled into Mrs. Sanders' throat burning the back of her tongue. Mrs. Sanders shuddered and tried to gather her breath. Peter grasped her hand and squeezed. She looked down at Peter, his brown eyeliner-colored chin quivered. Tears filled Mrs. Sanders' eyes, but she could not speak.

"So Peter, what do you think? I can give you anything you want. What do you want?"

Peter turned and looked at the devil, "Do you know what I want?"

"Yes, I do, Peter. I know exactly what you want."

"No, Peter! Do not follow the devil," Mrs. Sanders blurted out.

"I told you to be quiet, Rhonda Sanders!" Satan sneered pointing a bony finger at her. "I will now reveal to Peter why he should not listen to you! Why no one should listen to you! If those little children and their parents knew about you, Rhonda Sanders, those families would not want their children in your classroom."

Mrs. Sanders jolted awake. Her heart raced. She looked over to her clock radio; the red numbers blinked 3:20.

She rolled over and stared at the ceiling hoping sleep would creep back into her.

At 4:13, Mrs. Sanders got up and showered. By 5:30 Mrs. Sanders was in her classroom.

The day moved in twenty-minute increments: reading,

science, PE, recess, math, lunch, writing, math again, recess, and finally social studies. She took her class to the busses and then went back to her room. She picked a few items off the floor, put the chairs on top of the desks, moved the daily number, and collapsed in her chair.

Mrs. Sanders wanted to quit, to pack up her apartment and leave it all behind. She remembered feeling this way before, but she had never felt so incapable of helping her students. She no longer cared if they learned their math facts, she didn't care if they learned new words to read, and she didn't even care if their penmanship improved. None of it mattered.

Mrs. Sanders stood up and walked over to the closet where she had hung Peter's robe the day before, put her hand on the closet door, and closed her eyes. She bowed her head and prayed for a miracle. For the little boy dressed as Jesus to come out of the tomb and heal her. She opened the creaky door.

Peter's purple robe hung lifelessly in the dark space. She reached out and grasped the robe; spiny plant seeds fell from the hem of the fabric as she tugged the robe off the hanger. She lifted the dirty hem towards her face and stared at the dust and dried seeds. She shook the robe. Particles of desert dust and plant seeds fell to the floor. Mrs. Sanders shook the robe again. More sand and seeds floated to the floor. She stood looking at the mess on the floor. Tears fell from her eyes mixing with the dust.

She found the broom and swept the dust and seeds into a pile. She pushed the dry earth into a dustpan, carried it over to the sink area and sprinkled all of it into the class terrarium. She reached into the terrarium and pushed the seeds deep into the soil with her forefinger. She sprinkled water over the dried, dead things and hoped life would spring from the Earth again.

JON EEKHOFF

My Favorite Street Corner

My favorite street corner
Is lined with lazy chairs
Facing the street indifferently.

My favorite street corner
Is filled with people
Watching the world.

My favorite street corner
Is best visited in short sleeves
On a summer night.

My Sister Is A Space Alien

I believe my older sister Kay is a space alien. I reached this conclusion because there is no way we both came from the same gene pool, and she is not the type of person you would say was immaculately conceived. Not that she isn't a good person, but I just can't see my mom being a vessel for anything too holy.

Kay lives in El Salvador, where she is saving the world, at least that is what I tell people when they ask, "El Salvador? Why does she live there?" Explaining that answer is far too complicated, so saving the world allows the questioner to fill in the blanks.

Why would anyone leave the comfort of the United States to live in El Salvador? Mental illness is always a possibility, but I can assure you that Kay is somewhat sane. There was a time during college when I wondered if she had gone off the deep end. She lived in a house I termed "the commie house" with other students who had traveled to third world countries and returned to the US with an appropriate amount of guilt for being an American. I visited her once while she lived in the "commie house." It was the kind of place that gives you the creeps if you thought Ronald Reagan would make a better president than Walter Mondale.

Kay didn't start off saving the world. She started off going to elementary school, getting good grades, and wanting gumdrop glasses. She played sports (not very well), liked boys, and started using big words much too early for a child.

Junior high is when I noticed that my sister was pretty smart. It was straight As city for her, while I did my best to put forth as little effort as possible to get Bs and Cs. She ran for student body offices and won because she was the smartest kid and other kids thought that would be a bonus for political office (too bad that doesn't translate to the national stage). She still played volleyball, basketball and ran track, but again, she was not a natural athlete. She was too analytical to be a great athlete; you could almost see her making decisions before she did it, which never really works in fast-paced team sports.

When we moved to New Zealand for a year it hit me that my sister is a space alien. I spent the first week of school in a complete fog. I had no idea about anything these New Zealander kids were learning. They were in their fourth year of French; I had heard of France. They were doing advanced Algebra; I had no idea where this x in my math equation came from. Every class I went to was more confusing than the next. Even PE was confusing to me. Cricket? Rugby? Soccer? They called track athletics, they ran miles and miles, they played a game called netball; we even spent days taking tests and notes on physiology when I would have been out playing dodgeball in the US.

My sister had no problem with any of the classes. She learned fifth year French. She did the math. She wrote. She did homework and studied. I decided to become a juvenile delinquent. I hung around with the wrong crowd, tried smoking, lifted girl's skirts, and got kicked out of French class.

The seeming ease with which she made this transition did not amaze me at the time. It just made me mad. She was making me look bad. I was never going to put forth the effort to get straight As, and it would have been nice if my sister would have helped the family effort of slacking, but it just wasn't in her space alien genes.

When we came back to the States nothing changed, Kay got straight As; I did as little as possible. Teachers expected me to be like my sister; I'm sure most of them were disappointed. I did my work, but I would never sink low enough to study. Kay studied every night.

When she ran for a student body office it didn't surprise me. I assumed she would win and slowly begin taking over the known world. In her first attempt, she tied with the guy she ran against. I don't remember what office she was running for, but I know she tied. I remember this small fact because I didn't vote (information that didn't go over too well at home).

Thinking back, I'm not sure why I didn't vote. It might have been that I had something important to do, but it was probably because I had to decide whether I should go vote or get in the lunch line early. Lunch was a huge priority in my life, and I wasn't about to skip it to go to the polling area.

Kay didn't give me much grief, but my parents gave it to me with gusto. Maybe they realized that the fate of all of mankind rested on this election. If Kay did not win the election she might have gone into a deep depression and started using IV drugs. She was fated to win the election, and therefore won in a run-off.

Her rise to power began.

In Kay's senior year she was student body president, she was valedictorian, she earned a 4.0 GPA, and my life as a student was a living hell. By now most of the teachers knew not to expect me to be my sister, but my parents assumed I should be getting the same grades as Kay. They figured since we came from the same gene pool, we should get similar grades. What they didn't realize was that my sister is a space alien.

Kay's high school graduation prepared me for future embarrassing graduations to come. Who got to speak? Kay. Who got the most awards? Kay. Who looked like a fricking Christmas tree with all her awards strung around her neck? Kay. Who was going to look like a big loser next year because he had done nothing? Me.

When Kay ventured off to college, I missed her. I wrote to her a few times, but most of the time, I was too busy. I had sporting events to attend, girls to date, lies to tell my parents, incredibly stupid stunts to attempt and classes to barely pass. When it was time for me to choose a college, I decided to apply to the same college that Kay was attending hoping that her reputation would get me in under the line, and it did. It was no Ivy League school, and I don't even know why she decided to attend. She could have gone just about anywhere.

That summer we both worked at a church camp near Yosemite. I cleaned dishes, recycled cans, and cleaned toilets. I enjoyed cleaning the toilets most, people left me alone, and I had a fair amount of unsupervised time to goof off. Kay, on the other hand, had the responsible job of being a lifeguard. Away from school Kay was a normal person and therefore, infinitely more human in my mind. When she didn't have to study, or worry about school, she relaxed. She was still wound as tight as a rock-star's jeans, but she managed to have fun occasionally.

When I went off to college it was strange. Most kids spend their entire teen years longing to get away from their parents, and then when it happens they get a little scared. I was no different. Kay helped me pick classes, and I would see her around at times, but most often, she was studying. Needless to say, I was not studying. I was doing everything my parents forbid me from doing while I was living at home. When the first semester was over, I was hanging on by the skin of my academic teeth. Kay cruised through with straight As again and then left to go to school in Mexico.

I really don't know why Mexico was calling her name, but apparently it was. She got straight As. Even though everything was in Spanish, she got straight As. I had enough trouble with school in my own language.

When she got back, she showed me pictures, but it didn't help me understand why she went or anything else about the whole "school in Mexico" thing. Looking back on it now I can see how Mexico changed my sister's life.

For the longest time I assumed my sister would take over the world through the political process, but after her time in Mexico I sensed a change in her approach to world domination. Instead of taking over the world, she was now going to save the world. My focus was solely on saving money for the weekends. Saving the world was far beyond my hopes and dreams, but for Kay it was a possibility.

The next year Kay was off to Central America. She went with a group from the college of about twenty people. All of those people would return to our college changed. I don't know what they saw, but when they came back to the US they were different.

Reagan was president, Iran-Contra had yet to be discovered, and countries like El Salvador, Nicaragua, and Guatemala were on the evening news each night. These small countries, which most people in the US had never heard of before, were now places we heard of but never wanted to visit. Aside from the poverty, random violence, and disease, it sounded like an okay place to get a tan.

The Central American group, or as I liked to call them "the commies," had an opportunity to present what they had learned on the trip to the entire college in a weekly class called Forum. To me Forum was like a good dose of Nyquil and I spent most of my time wondering how I would get to lunch early.

The day the "commies" presented was entertaining if your sister wasn't the one on-stage crying. Kay told a story about a guy who was shot for doing something to an American flag. The whole story escaped me, but she said, "And they killed him for a piece of cloth," and then started crying. I was horrified. Not horrified as I should have been that some idiot had killed someone over the flag, but I was horrified that my sister was on stage crying, embarrassing me.

A few years later, my friend Eric's sister embarrassed him in a similar manner, and we decided we should form a support group of guys embarrassed during Forum by their sisters. It would be a small group, but isn't that what people said about Jesus and his Disciples?

Kay finished her undergraduate degree with a 4.0 GPA. They gave her a trophy called the president's cup and recognized her during the ceremony as an outstanding student. There would be no such recognition for me; in fact, I didn't attend my graduation because the Lakers were playing the Jazz in the playoffs, and I couldn't miss the game on TV. A man must have his priorities.

After graduation Kay was off to choose from hundreds of jobs, I assumed, but she ended up taking a position as a lifeguard for the YMCA in Seattle. It confused me a bit that all the effort in school would amount to watching kids secretly pee in a pool in Seattle, but Kay always marched to her own freeform jazz band.

After the summer came to a close, she started working as a paralegal helping Central American refugees. I am not sure what she did. I don't know if she did translating, or their dishes, I just know when people asked me I gave them the answer, "She is a paralegal working with Central Americans." Often the people asking about her would want me to pass on a hug or a "Hi" and I always said I would, but never did.

What she did in Seattle didn't interest me as much as what she had in her refrigerator.

Once, when I was visiting, I looked in her fridge and saw she had gourmet ketchup. It seemed extravagant to me to have gourmet ketchup, but I longed to have a job where I could buy gourmet ketchup. I was still a destitute college student who stole all his toilet paper from the library and got all his ketchup from fast food restaurant bins. Kay having gourmet ketchup was a bit of a paradox: here was a girl/lady who spent her days and nights helping people who were escaping horrible situations in their countries and somewhere in her day she thought, "I would really like some gourmet ketchup. I will have to pick some of that up on the way home." It just didn't fit: fighting for justice against the huge military industrial machine and consumer of gourmet ketchup.

After her experience in Seattle, she decided to move to Los Angeles and do her paralegaling there. Los Angeles was the Mecca of Central American refugees, and she would be kept busy there I figured.

She got a job working for an organization called El Rescate, and even with my limited Spanish, I knew what that meant.

The next part of the story is the most improbable part; it is the part where Kay falls in love with a guy at work.

Kay had dated a number of guys, each one of them a loser in some way or another, but she never seemed too interested in them. I discovered one guy reading with her when I dropped by her dorm room unannounced. He was reading *Shogun,* and she was probably reading some book with a title longer than this sentence. I teased her relentlessly about how this guy was reading her the dirty parts of *Shogun* when I interrupted. I'm sure the whole thing was perfectly innocent, but Kay blushed, nevertheless.

When Kay fell in love, my wife and I drove down to LA to meet the new guy and find out what made him so special. We all got together at the International House of Pancakes, which seemed oddly appropriate because Kay was saving the world, and IHOP is all about making the world a better place through pancakes.

Oscar, the object of my sister's love, was not what I had expected. I had pictured some bookish-brainiac type; Oscar was a warm, engaging, smart, funny guy. His smile made you feel comfortable and welcomed. We talked over pancakes and coffee and then went back to their office where we found out Oscar was the boss.

He had escaped from El Salvador and come to the US. He didn't have all the 4.0 nonsense my sister had, but he had done some incredible things since arriving in LA. He met movie stars, politicians, movie stars who were politicians, politicians who thought they should be movie stars, and various other big shots. All of his schmoozing was done so he could get money to help Central American refugees. After spending three hours with Oscar, I decided he was probably a space alien, too, but a nice space alien sent to help us on planet Earth.

The strangest part of the day was when Kay and Oscar told us that they were expecting a baby.

Now I had a very difficult time seeing my sister as a mother. I could imagine this poor kid bringing home a B+ on his first-grade report card and getting sent to his room with no food. The poor kid would never get to play sports or go outside until he had done all of his homework and read one book each day, but as it turns out, my sister and Oscar are very good parents, who now have three nice, well-adjusted kids, as far as I can tell.

After Kay had her first son, she finished her MA at UCLA, with a 4.0, and got some special "service to the community award" recognition at graduation, again. Some day she will get her PhD and put me to shame again, but that is a future embarrassment for which I will have to wait.

Kay and Oscar moved their family to El Salvador twenty-five years ago and started saving the world from a more centralized location. They talk occasionally about returning to the US, but I think they are very happy there. I imagine it is easier to see progress in El Salvador than it is in the US, and therefore the work is more satisfying.

Or it could be that the space aliens on the mother ship get less radio interference when contacting my sister.

The Worst Paperboy Ever

I was probably the worst paperboy of all time.

It all started when a junior high neighborhood kid, who was several years older than me and quite cool as I remember him, wanted to quit his paper route. I was enamored with the idea that I could become a paperboy, earn a little money, and become cool like the neighborhood kid. Unfortunately, like most of my early plans in life, this one failed.

Before I was awarded this fantastic employment opportunity, the cool kid allowed me to follow him on his route for a week. I would meet him at his house after school each day, and we would fold the papers, put them in the paperboy bag, and then ride the route together. He had the entire route memorized and knew a little about each of the customers. This impressed me to no end. Here was this kid who was so smart he had memorized his entire route of nearly two hundred customers. This feat was not so impressive after I began the monotonous process of riding this same route every day, tossing papers to the same people over and over and over, but at the time, I was in awe.

The kid rode his bike with ease. He tossed each paper with a flick of the wrist, and each paper floated onto the porch of the house. If he did miss I was happy to run onto the yard, grab the paper and place it on the porch, much like a trained dog. This on-the-job training was the best part of my paperboy experience; it was the only time when I was able to live in my dream world where everything made sense. In my mind I would soon take over the route, ride my orange Sears Spyder bike with ease and flick papers that would drift softly onto the welcome mats of my customers. Unfortunately, the real world had a way of intruding into my daydream world, and when my training period ended, I had no idea which houses were paying customers and which were not.

I didn't have a clue where to start. I hadn't thought about it until the first day I was on my own, riding my bike down the street, loaded with papers, looking for the first house. Suddenly, the whole idea of being a paperboy didn't seem so glamorous; in fact, it was frightening.

My fifth-grade mind came up with a plan. I decided to toss the papers to random houses and hope for the best. So, I rode confidently down the street tossing papers at every third house. If someone was in the yard, I studied them carefully to see if they looked like they were expecting a paper. Anyone who made a movement toward me got a paper; if they looked away, I rode on with coolness. Somehow it all made sense to me, and I really thought there would be no problems.

When I approached the Country Club apartment complex my confidence was finally shaken. The twelve apartment buildings all looked the same. They were the same color of awful green; they all had the same bushes and the same kind of lawn. The Country Club apartments were as close to a slum as my small city could offer. It would be years before I could equate anything positive with the term "country club."

I thought about bluffing my way around the apartment complex as I had done with the first part of my route, but I feared that I might toss a paper on some illiterate's doorstep, and he would take insult, chase me down and beat me to death for mocking him with a newspaper. Instead of risking bodily harm, I made an executive decision and rode through the complex and delivered exactly zero newspapers.

Again, this seemed the most logical thing to do then, but today it seems like one of those bizarre dreams where you do completely illogical things for no apparent reason.

Most of the Country Club people were Navy families with kids whose fathers were missing because they were in Vietnam working on jets. The Naval Air Station was close to Lemoore about three miles west of my house. There were lots of squadrons with names like "Strike Fighter Squadron 151" for my friends' dads who were somewhere far away near Vietnam on Conventionally-Powered Aircraft Carriers or Nuclear-Powered Aircraft Carriers like the USS Enterprise or USS Forrestal. All of it was confusing to me. Just looking at papers was difficult enough. Most of my friends would see their dads every few months when the men were home for about two weeks before disappearing again. I worried because women did not allow my slacky job.

As I neared the end of my route a sudden revelation hit me. I had about twenty papers left. I was a block from my house, and I knew that arriving home with twenty papers would be a bad thing. My mom would certainly have a few pointed questions and would say responsibility about fifty times in the span of three sentences.

The solution was a simple one; I rode up to a garbage can a block from my house and dumped the contents of my paper bag into the can. Problem solved.

The next day there were a number of complaints stacked on the bundle of papers that were delivered to my house. I noted the addresses of the complaints and made a mental note to make sure I got papers to those addresses. The sheer brilliance of this plan pleased me a great deal. I would slowly build the list of customers from my list of complaints. Each day I might add five or ten "new" customers to my pretend route and eventually I would have something resembling the actual route I inherited.

I still had the problem each day of disposing of a number of papers. I began hiding them in bushes, tossing them to houses not on my route. I would toss complaining customers two papers to make up for the one they missed the day before. I even stuffed a bunch down a sewer drain. Eventually all my hard work was noticed by the newspaper office, and I got a call from the distribution center. I was never an expert liar but, in this case, I made a pretty rock-solid case against the previous paperboy and his inability to train me. The next day I had a complete list of paying customers.

Those houses that spent a week on my imaginary route were probably disappointed, but now I was free to screw up my job in so many other ways.

It didn't take me long to discover that once I had the list of customers that was equal to the number of papers I had to deliver, I was in trouble. In the past, if I tossed a paper somewhere inconveniently, I could always pull one from my surplus and give it a second try. Now if I gave it a second try, I would run out of papers before I ran out of houses, which meant I got to head home early, but for my customers at the end of the route, it meant they would get no paper.

My first month on the job finally came to an end, and with the end of the month came collections. The whole concept of collections now seems ridiculous to me. The newspaper office would send me, the weakest link in the chain, out to collect money for the month's papers. I would arrive to collect money; people would blow me off and I would go to the next house. I stuffed money from collections in my pockets, in my paper bag, in my socks, anyplace that would soon drift from my mind and be lost. The money was one problem, but facing my angry customers was a whole other issue.

There was no one else to blame for tossing a paper on the roof, or on a yard that was being watered, or under a bush, or cracking a window with an ill-advised toss. Each door I knocked on would bring me more surprises and examples of my incompetence. Sometimes these folks were angry, other times they just listed off a series of complaints and then paid the bill. I offered no excuse for my job performance; I just stood there taking the abuse like an expressionless painting of a paperboy who didn't really care. There were a couple people that expected me to refund them for each paper that was not delivered or had been destroyed through some fault of mine, and I happily refunded their money and never gave it a second thought.

One older lady requested her paper to be porched each day. She had trouble walking out to her yard to get her paper, but she also had a large dog that was tied to her porch that terrified me. Whenever I rode my bike within twenty feet of the dog it would become a crazed ball of fur, teeth and froth. There was no way I was going to get anywhere near the porch, and there was no way I could guarantee the paper would end up on the porch. The older lady told me she would happily tip me fifty cents a month for my extra effort, but I told her that her dog scared me and getting her paper where she wanted it was physically impossible. She gave me an ultimatum: either get the paper on the porch or she'd cancel her subscription. I'm sure she wanted me to suddenly change my mind and promise to get her paper on the porch, but one less paper delivery had certain appeal to me. I canceled her paper on the spot, walked back to my bike, and rode off. She stood in her doorway with her mouth open as I whistled down the street.

Of all the problems dogging me, the one that I could never shake was the last guy on my route. If his paper wasn't there by 5 o'clock my parents got a call. I tried everything I could think of to please him, except the obvious solutions of going a little faster or starting my route with his house and going backwards. For some reason I found the best solution was to toss the newspaper at his metal garage door as hard as I could. The impact made a noise like thunder. This did little to please my customer, but if he wanted to know when his paper would arrive, he now had a system to announce, "Your paper is here!"

I continued this abuse of his garage until it was time to face the victim of my abuse at the end of the month. He let me know that my efforts were not appreciated and that he would contact the office if I continued to use his garage door like I was Keith Moon. I stopped the gonging the following day but found a more interesting way to annoy him.

This fellow had a set of white double doors that served as my next target. The first day I smashed the paper right against the door with a satisfying thud, but what really pleased me more than the noise was the black mark the paper left on the white door. As the month wore on, I found that I didn't even have to throw the paper with much steam to get a pretty good mark on his door, and when it was time to collect that month's bill his once white doors were blackened by my accurate tosses. He complained again, but this time I had a ready-made excuse. "I was just trying to make sure you got your paper on the porch." Now how can you be mad at a paperboy who was doing his best to do his job?

He was obviously still angry, but there was nothing he could say other than to request that I toss the paper on the porch without damaging his door. It was a small victory, but a victory nevertheless. Customer service has never been a gift of mine.

From that point on I really tried to land the paper, without incident, on the porch. It became a small point of pride with me; some people might even say I had matured, but really I developed a fantasy world where I competed against the best paperboys from around the world. Most of the time the contest came down to the last toss and if I landed it, the USA would be victorious over the Russian paperboys again. If I did miss the porch, there was always some judge's ruling that placed the victory in the USA's hands. These technicalities were a bit convoluted, but as I saw it we owed them one for the 1972 Olympic basketball loss.

It was during one of these victory celebrations that I was almost killed: when I say, "almost killed," I guess I mean very nearly killed or if things had gone horribly wrong I would have died.

It was a Friday, and on Fridays the papers were a little heavier due to various supplements that were inserted, so they were much easier to toss, and the wind would not blow them on a roof or into a window.

As I came to the final ten houses on my route, I imagined I was pitted in one of the toughest newspaper boy contests of all time. The free world was depending on my ability to land the final ten papers on the porches of the final ten houses. This scenario had been played out before, but I usually screwed it up within two or three houses. This Friday was different though. Each paper left my hand with a little magic touch. I didn't start to feel the pressure until I reached house number seven. My breathing was a little forced, I could feel my hands shaking, and I had to pick up the intensity a bit. My focus paid off as I hit the porches of the seventh, eighth and ninth houses. It all came down to one final throw. Howard Cosell was doing color commentary in my head as I approached the final house and let loose the paper. It darted through the air and landed without a bounce on the front door mat. The celebration in my head sent electrical impulses into my arms and I raised my balled fists in victory. The crowd went wild, and I was the hero of the Western world.

This celebration ended suddenly as I saw a brown Trans Am speeding directly toward me. At the last moment the car slid sideways, a la Starsky and Hutch, and hit me broadside sending me flying off my bike and onto the sidewalk.

A high school kid jumped out of the driver's door and pounced on me. Grabbing my T-shirt with both hands he shook me while shouting, "If I ever see you pointing that finger at me again, I will break it off." I wasn't really terrified; I was more confused than terrified. Did this guy know me?

Was he confusing me with someone else? What finger was he worried about? I even wondered if my dream world was slipping into reality and this guy was a Russian spy who was upset with my successful completion of ten porches in a row.

As he let me go and drove off, I wished I was Bruce Banner so when the high school kid grabbed me, I could have said, "You're making me mad. You won't like me when I'm mad." Then I would have turned into the Hulk, tossed him onto the porch, picked up his car and snapped it in half on my knee, and ridden my bike home in my Hulk form.

The more I thought about it, the cooler I thought it would be if I was the Hulk riding my bike. I wondered how far the Hulk could ride with one push of the pedal. I picked up my bike, still in character, and got ready to find out how far the Hulk could go on one push. I moved the right-side pedal to the top and prepared to see just what the Hulk could do. I put all my weight on my right foot and pushed as hard as I could. My Hulk-like strength was focused on this one push and when my foot slipped off the pedal I went head over handlebars. The ensuing crash would have been hilarious to watch on videotape, but videotape had not been invented yet, so the crash took place without much notice.

My knee hit the asphalt first, then my shoulder and finally my chin. I was sprawled out in the middle of the street like some idiot pretending to be the Hulk who wasn't quite up to the task. I picked myself up and brushed off the pieces of rock that were now imbedded in my flesh and watched the blood flow from my leg. Just as I was about to have myself a nice sit-down cry, a car pulled up with a very concerned looking middle-aged woman at the wheel. "Are you all right?" she asked.

Even though I was just in the fifth grade I knew the rules of being a man. No matter how bad it hurts, you never admit it hurts. "I'm fine," I said as blood dripped from my chin onto my shirt.

"Are you sure you are okay? What happened?" she asked again.

"I'm fine. I do stuff like this all the time," I replied, which was probably closer to the truth than I wanted to be, but you can't just say, "I was pretending to be the Hulk and my foot slipped off the pedal, and because of the incredible force harnessed in the Hulk's legs, I fell like a rotten apple from a tree."

I straightened my bike's handlebars and hopped back on. As I was riding home trying to ignore the burning pain, I could feel my flip-flop begin to stick to the bottom of my foot as the blood ran down my leg to pool on it. There was a satisfying smacking from this stickiness, a stickiness that I began to enjoy. It might have been the only thing I enjoyed in my time as a paperboy.

This may be why I netted about negative $50 for my year and a half of work.

Mike's Teddy

I
Felt the guilt,
When she
Dropped the teddy
Into the
Burn barrel.

I
Watched the flames consume
One of three
Objects from my
Brother's past.
Connecting him to an
Unknown family.
The smoke rose signaling
A new beginning and
An end.

I
Felt the guilt.

Cemetery Boy

The largest, greenest space in my hometown was the city cemetery. At one time it sat outside the city boundaries, but the town grew around it. The number of times I went onto the grounds as a youngster could be counted on one hand, but I would pass the large square block of green grass and distant gray headstones every time I went anywhere.

One day my father came home from a funeral and told me that there was a summer job at the cemetery. Two days later I was employed.

I wasn't sure what I would be doing there, but as I found out, there were always things to do. The foreman, Van, seemed to be obsessed with the idea that we might be seen not working, so if there was ever free time between 8 am and 5 pm, Van would find the crew something to do.

Monday was mowing day, all day. Three of us would mow, and one of us, usually me, would use the hand-shears to trim the bushes that dotted the cemetery ground. It was not backbreaking work, but it was incredibly monotonous. The hand-shears turned a job that could have been done in two hours with a power trimmer into an all-day extravaganza of boredom.

Tuesday was edging day. All four of us would get gas-powered weed-eaters, and we would spend the day edging around the headstones. After about an hour my brain would go numb. Over and over again I would cut the grass touching the headstones. After all the headstones were done, we would sweep the grass off every cement surface in the entire cemetery.

Wednesday was maintenance day. That meant cleaning the mowers, sharpening the blades, changing the oil in the machines, and generally keeping busy.

Thursday was mowing again. During the height of summer, mowing twice a week was needed to keep the grass looking good.

Friday was the only day that provided any variety in the schedule, and that was not necessarily a good thing. A day without a plan meant a day under Van's thumb. Van seemed to enjoy his power and drew a perverse pleasure in assigning incredibly boring or difficult tasks.

Burials were our only hope to break the monotony of days. Burials meant dropping everything, playing with big toys, standing around in the shade, and a change in schedule.

Setting up for a funeral took a great deal of planning and time. The day before the funeral, we would water the plot where the hole would be dug. This watering softened the soil and made the grass easier to cut and remove. The sod needed to be carefully removed and set aside, so that it could be returned to its proper place after the casket was in the ground.

After the sod was cut, we would dig the hole. If we could get the backhoe into the area, we would use it, or I should say,

Van would use the backhoe. No one else was allowed to touch the backhoe. It was Van's holy relic that only he was allowed to touch. We would lay out plywood for Van to park the backhoe on; the plywood was set down to make sure the area around the grave was not damaged. Van would then sit atop his throne and scoop out "spoonfuls" of dirt and plop them down next to the stack of sod. Once the grave started to get deep one of us would have to jump down into it and smooth out the sides with a square shovel. The shovel was then used to measure the depth of the grave. The shovel was five feet long and that was the depth all the graves were dug to, not the advertised six feet under.

The last bit of heavy work was dropping a vault into the grave. A vault is a large cement case that the casket would be placed into. The vault's main purpose was to prevent the ground from sinking, but it also preserved the caskets and added a few thousand dollars to the bill.

When all the dirt was scooped and the grave was ready, it was time to beautify the funeral area. We would cover all the exposed dirt with AstroTurf. The pile of dirt was covered, the graveside was covered and anything that might remind someone that their loved one was about to be placed into the dirt was hidden. I thought it all looked very tacky, but it was what we did.

Then we would set up chairs, get the metal cart that the casket would be set on, and wheel out the portable canopy to shade the family and casket. Once everything was in place and met Van's approval, we could move on to our regular schedule of work until the funeral car arrived.

We were instructed to drop everything as soon as people arrived and to make a straight line for the shop where we would sit like church mice, or at least that was what we were supposed to do. While most people assumed all of this activity would be done solemnly and with a great deal of reverence, it was not. There was plenty of laughter, teasing, and talk while the set up was done, and once the funeral started Romero would always sneak out, look through the bushes and check out the young women.

In the shop we would get Van to tell us stories about his instant hot water faucet. We spent hours asking serious sounding questions like, "Can you make tea with your instant hot water? What about instant chicken soup? Have you ever tried washing your hands in the instant hot water? Do you think you could cook noodles with the instant hot water? What if you filled your sink up, could you cook noodles then?" Van took each question seriously and answered with a pained expression, like he was working on quantum physics. Later when we were away from Van we would replay the discussions for laughs. Romero delighted in these discussions and never tired of calling Van colorful names and planning new absurd questions.

Once the funeral was over and all the people left, we would congregate around the casket and begin picking up all the chairs, AstroTurf, and funeral stuff. Lowering the casket was easy unless something went wrong with the crank that lowered the box. One time the crank got stuck, and we were forced to slide the ropes off one end before the casket was all the way to the bottom. The freed end of the casket smashed into the vault with a huge clank. The foot end of the casket hovered about two feet from the ground, and I heard the body slide to the low end of the casket, coming to rest with a thud.

I never thought about the bodies inside the boxes. It just didn't seem real or important. To all of us on the crew, there were no bodies just boxes, dirt and grass, but after hearing the body slump to one end of the box, I could not help but imagine how the body inside was all scrunched up with his head and arms filling the low end of the box. Romero and I actually spent some time imitating the position to each other later that day. It was funny, in a kind of sick way.

Once we had the vault lid on, we would then begin the process of tossing the dirt back in the grave and tamping it down. One of us would be sent to do other chores while the other two finished off the job.

When the summer started to really heat up, the number of funerals increased. During August, it was common to have a funeral each day, and some days there were double or even triple funerals. A double funeral day was like a paid vacation for us. We could barely keep ahead of the funerals and spent a good two hours sitting in the shop.

We rarely talked about death or the people who died. Death was more an abstract idea than a reality, which is more than a little odd if you consider death surrounded us on all sides, yet death surrounds us all on all sides, and we go through life thinking as little about it as possible.

There were two sets of headstones that intrigued me. One set was a mother who died on December 17, 1969 along with her four children. They were buried next to each other under one large headstone. Each time I passed the headstone I would try to imagine what might have happened. Was there a house fire that killed all of them? Was it murder? I spent some time thinking about the possibilities after work when I had idle time.

After a month of wondering, I asked Bob, who had worked there for the longest time. Bob said it had been a car accident. A large truck carrying dairy cows crossed the center lane of the highway in the fog and ran directly into the car. They were all killed instantly. I never wondered about the headstone again.

The other set of headstones was a father and son who died on the same day. The son was thirty when he died, and the father was fifty-seven. Bob would not give me a straight answer about the deaths, other than to say they had been shot. He said he couldn't remember. I imagined that it must have been some kind of shoot-out with a criminal.

I finally asked Romero if he knew what had happened, and his answer was right out of a Greek tragedy. I was sure Romero was joking, but I approached Bob one day with Romero's story. Bob confirmed that there was a love triangle involving the mother/wife. The men killed each other. Needless to say, each time I passed the headstone, a series of disturbing thoughts passed through my head.

Eventually all the headstones were the same to me: large cement slabs of names, dates, and clichés carved into the stone. The names meant nothing to me, the dates meant nothing to me, and the clichés seemed especially unoriginal and trite.

Late one evening the phone rang at my home. My mom picked it up. I could hear her saying, "Unhun. Unhun, mmm. Okay." Right after she hung up she walked into my room and told me that Jeff Hess, a friend of mine, had died in a car accident.

I didn't know what to say, so I just answered, "Okay." It was a surreal moment; I had talked to Jeff hours before. It had been all "jock" talk, a series of insults exchanged about mothers, sports heroes and anything else that could embarrass the other guy. It was the same conversation I had with all of my teammates when I would run into them around town, but this conversation was now important.

The next day I was back at work.

Two days later, I was standing in the cemetery looking at Jeff's casket sitting amidst the AstroTurf. This time I was one of the guests, dressed in slacks and a tie. The heat of the day was oppressive.

I could see Romero peeking through the bushes near the shop. I didn't want him there. I wanted him to respect my friends. I wanted him to respect the sanctity of Jeff's funeral. I wanted to drift off into the breeze and not return.

Work hadn't changed. I had.

Families

Mark lifted the office chair out of the bed of the truck and set it gently on the cold asphalt. He hadn't really thought too much about how he was going to get the chair home. He just knew he was taking it.

He placed his suitcase in the chair's seat and rolled it toward the rental car office. The roar of the wheels might have amused him on another day, but nothing in Wichita amused Mark on this trip.

He mentally scrolled through his five days in Kansas: airport, funeral home, Dad's apartment, Emily's house, funeral home, church, cemetery, Emily's home, the big blow-up, and now back to the airport. Why Dad decided to move out here with Emily still puzzled Mark. Nothing but gray skies, empty trees, dirty mounds of snow, and Republican bumper stickers. It was not the place he pictured his father spending his last years on the planet.

The retirement community in San Diego where Dad had lived with Mom was ideal, surrounded by orange trees and white stucco bungalows. Eighty degrees every day, blue skies and lots of other retired couples to play golf and tennis with. After Mom died Dad didn't want to stay in San Diego.

Kansas was cheap compared to San Diego. Wichita had a retirement home by the river, but it reminded Mark of the apartment complex where he used to deliver newspapers, the place his Mom told him to deliver the papers first, before it got dark.

Mark pushed the chair through the glass door and into the rental agency.

"Good evening sir. Are you here to return your vehicle?" the young lady behind the counter asked.

"Yep."

"And what is your last name, sir?" Mark paused not able to remember the answer to a question he had known most of his life.

"Benz, Mark Benz."

She fingered through a pile of pink documents "Here you are. Heading back home to Portland tonight?"

"Yeah, Portland," Mark said as he mechanically signed the paperwork and slid it back to the agent. She began punching away at the computer's keys, and Mark looked at her, really looked at her. She had that Kansas look about her, evangelical hair, 1950s bra, and just a little too much make-up.

She looked up, "What'cha doing with the chair?"

"I'm taking it home with me."

"On the plane?"

"No, I thought I would roll it there."

"That's funny."

"Yah, I'm a regular Chris Rock."

"Who?"

"Chris Rock..."

"Oh, I guess I don't know him. Is he funny?"

"Really funny if you like the word fuck." Mark pounced on the word, punching it into her. She did not smile and went back to her keyboard. Mark noticed tears building in her eyes.

"Here you are sir," she said handing the finished paperwork to him before clearing her right eye with her hand.

Mark tossed the papers onto his father's chair, turned and pushed the chair toward the airport terminal.

***

"Did ya catch the chair thing?" Ian asked.

"No, what chair thing?" Kathy asked.

"Okay, so Dad bought this chair for Grandpa a couple years ago and it sounds like Emily didn't want Dad to take it."

"No, I didn't hear that one. When did you hear that?"

"Get me another beer out of the mini-fridge and I'll tell you all about it."

Kathy got up off the hotel bed and went over to the mini-fridge. "What kind do you want?"

"Get me one of the stout ones."

"One of the fat bottles?"

"No, one of the stout beers, the ones with the monk on the label."

"Oh, here you go. Now tell me about the chair."

"Alright, so you know when Jack's mom came over to the house?"

"Well, I was in the living room looking at Emily's museum when Jack's mom arrived. Did you see all of the collectables that Emily is taking?"

"No, I didn't go in there."

"There must be a million dollars worth of Indian artifacts in that room, Ian. I mean it. There are pots like the ones in the DeYoung museum in San Francisco. I saw an Antique Roadshow once where this old lady brought in a rug just like three that Emily has hanging on the wall. The guy on the show said the rug would be worth $50,000…and Emily has three of them," Kathy said.

"So…"

"So, half of that stuff should be Dad's, but Emily says Grandma promised it all to her even though the will says Dad and Emily should split it. What we need is King Solomon. He'd know what to do," Kathy said. "Oh, yeah, what was the deal with the chair?"

"Okay, you know that crappy old office chair that Dad bought Grandpa?"

"Yeah."

"Well, Dad took it. I guess the Kansas side of the family isn't happy. When Jack's mom came in all the cousins were like, 'Where's Grandpa's chair?' and Jack was like, 'Mark took it.' They asked about twelve times and each time Jack said, 'Mark took it.' You'd think there wasn't another chair in Kansas. Where are they all going to sit once Dad leaves? Everyone in Kansas will be looking for a place to sit and asking, 'Wha' happen' ta tha' chair?' 'Oh, Mark took it.' Everybody in Kansas will have to spend the rest of their lives standing up because Dad took the chair."

***

Emily wanted to sit in Dad's chair, but it was gone. Mark had taken it, and she knew it was better just to let it go.

Emily looked at the dishes piled in the sink and considered leaving them. They would be there tomorrow. Everything would be here tomorrow except Dad. This emptiness caught her by surprise, and for a moment she felt weak. "No!" Emily said stomping her foot. She advanced through the ache, into the kitchen, and opened the dishwasher.

Mark got to fly in from Portland for Dad's last few days. Mark didn't do the work of death; he just arrived for the end. Where was Mark when Dad roamed the house looking for Mom? Where was Mark when Dad couldn't remember where he was? Where was Mark when Dad wanted to drive? Where was Mark? "Portland," Emily said aloud as she banged a pot into the bottom rack.

"I paid for the chair, and I'm taking it," Emily said jamming a plate into an open space. "It doesn't matter what you bought, Mark." Another plate hit the rack.

Mark got what he wanted, just like when they were young. Emily always took what was left. She wanted the chair; Mark got it. She wanted to move Dad to Portland; he stayed in Wichita. She wanted a traditional burial; Dad was cremated. She wanted Mark to say he was sorry for not being there for the past three years; she got accused of stealing the rugs, the pots, and the pictures.

Mark left, and Emily held her tongue. She packed in all of the years of second place and held on.

She finished packing the dishwasher, closed the door, and turned the dial to "Pots and Pans." The dishwasher came to life. A surging feeling crawled up Emily's legs and into her gut, tightening. She bent her knees, pressed her back against the dishwasher, and sat on the floor. She felt warm as the swelling sounds of water amplified. Emily drew her legs up to her chest and let out a long cavernous groan.

Esther Eekhoff

Photographs spilled out across a floor
Images from the past
I filter though looking for you.

Canada 1969
There you were, eternal to me
Together we stood in clean white aisles
Spurned by my parents, I turn to you.
A black bear piggy bank had me spellbound
We left the store together, hand in hand.
Bank tucked under my arm.

Arizona 1971
There you were your hair in curlers and pins.
Sitting in a Lazy Boy surrounded by eight grandchildren
(My last meeting with fair-haired Lance,
Soon to be stricken by Reyes Syndrome)
You bought me roller skates, in a time before helmets and pads.
We told jokes, your laughter spilled out of the cinder block
Room and down the hall.

Iowa 1974
There you were, standing with Grandpa in the DesMoines airport.
We drove through Iowa fields to the farm,
To begin my Huck Finn summer.
Chasing fireflies in open fields on muggy nights,
Continually tossing a ball on the shed roof,
Playing with plastic army men on red stairs,
Wheaties-- sandwiches and soup-- meat, potatoes and gravy
Scripture at each meal, church three times a week
You at the piano singing *The Old Rugged Cross*.

Pasadena 1985

There you were hair in curlers and pins.
You cooked me breakfast after everyone had eaten,
Eggs, hash browns, bacon and fresh orange juice squeezed
From a full fruit tree outside the front door.
I napped on the floor after eating.
We watched the parade on TV instead of walking three blocks.
You cried that night when you spoke to Mike,
Both of you reared without knowing your mothers.

Boise, Idaho 1987

There you were, waiting at the Greyhound station.
We spent a week together,
Not the Spring Break I had imagined.
I climbed a mountain too close to dinner time,
Wandered around the Reservation,
I even tried to ice fish with Grandpa,
But there were no Minnesota winters in my blood.
We ate the same meals, read the scripture and attended church

Two white owls sat motionless in a bare tree
Just outside your front door.
Unnoticed until I looked up,
My heart raced.
They remained unmoved.
Watching over,
There they were,
Fading into the background,
Always there,
Large eyes fixed on me.

Kansas 2001

There you were hair in curlers and pins.
Sitting in a Lazy Boy, surrounded by seven great-grandchildren.
Kronos had finally dug his fingers deep into you.
Your laugh still filled the room, but could not crawl down the
halls.
We talked. You told me I was your favorite, so were six others.
I cried during the celebration,
My musings welling up and overflowing.

The phone rang late one night,
You would be there no longer.
No longer eternal,
At least not in this world.

John

One day he came bursting through the classroom door demanding to write for the school newspaper. His hygiene, to be perfectly honest, was poor for someone in tenth grade. His blonde hair was long and unkempt. It swirled around his head and needed a good washing and combing. All of his clothing was dirty and ill-fitting, but the thing that bothered me most about John was his lack of interpersonal skill. He didn't exhibit any of the social norms for interacting with people. He stood too close, listened too little and was far too enthusiastic.

John was the kid we all knew from high school, the outcast. The kid that other kids made fun of and played dirty jokes on, the guy that never fit in no matter how hard he tried, and he really tried. He tried too hard and that drove his peers away even faster. He was a man aboard a sinking ship trying to convince other people to come on board.

I told him that he could write for the paper if he wanted, but he would get no credit for the class. He argued, a skill I found he had been practicing for most of his life on a daily basis. He wanted to get credit for writing, he wanted a large by-line, he wanted to be editor, he wanted to start a creative writing magazine, he wanted to run the world and have control of the entire universe. I gave him a small assignment and assumed I would not see him again. I was wrong.

He showed up the next day with a completed article for the school newspaper. He wanted to write more. I deflected his request and acted like I had things to do, as if I didn't have time to talk to him, but in reality I had plenty of time, just not the patience. It was a pattern I relied on when dealing with people that I really didn't want to deal with.

The problem with John was that he didn't pick up on those non-verbal hints most people would get. Either he chose to ignore the hints, or he just didn't interact with enough people to get the idea that he wasn't wanted. He just kept showing up.

These daily invasions became part of my life; John would stop by two or three times a day. Each time he would attempt to engage me in an argument. He was probing for an issue that would get me angry enough to fight. I remained distant and tried to avoid taking a side on any issue, but that didn't seem to deter him at all. He continued to push, doing all he could to inflame a discussion. There was a part of this little game that I enjoyed, but for the most part it was an annoyance. I longed to hide inside my classroom during break, although I was sure John would enter the room looking for me and begin his little game within the confines of my classroom.

Then one day John showed up after school. I was preparing for the next day's classes and had a good deal of work to get done. He came in and sat on one of the desks. "How can I be more popular?" he asked.

I was caught off-guard. I was so used to sparing with John that I was not prepared to have a real discussion. It took some time to find out what exactly John wanted from me. He just wanted to be liked, he wanted to be one of the guys, and he wanted to fit. I gave him some advice, but the realities of high school would never allow a person like John to just fit in and be one of the guys. He was disposed to be an outcast. He fit into the role; he just hadn't accepted it yet. There was a part of him that longed to be popular, but there was an even bigger part of him that drove him to offend and relish the role of class pariah.

As the year wore on, John annoyed me less as I became accustomed to his personality and his quirks. In fact, I began to find him an interesting person, and I started to enjoy his interruptions in my day.

There are times when I question my place in the world as a teacher. I have begun to believe my job is less about imparting knowledge and more about relationships with students. The idea of being a teacher who imparts knowledge down from a mountaintop just doesn't fit who I am or who my students seem to need me to be. Students connect with certain teachers and there is nothing you, as the teacher, can do about it. There are teachers at my school who make great connections with students who absolutely despise me, and those connections are important for those students to grow. We all want to be liked, but being liked is not part of the job, and being despised is the role a teacher must accept. As much as I wanted to connect with all my students early in my career, I have come to the realization that I must be consistent and fair in my decisions. At times those decisions alienate me from students, I have learned the most from people who held my feet to the fire and not let me get by. It is as if God has made a huge puzzle, and we are all looking for our specific place where we fit. John was a puzzle piece who fit with me, but I didn't want to acknowledge how well he fit or how much I liked him.

There are days when I look around my school and ask myself, "What am I doing here? How did I get here? Am I wasting my life here?" I have always felt a calling to teaching, but never really wanted to teach. As a student, I viewed the vast majority of my teachers as people who just couldn't cut it in the "real world." They wore old clothes, were out of touch with students and didn't seem to know much about anything interesting. They did not impress me at all; I did not aspire to be the next Mr. Kanatarude. Yet, I became a teacher. It was a choice I made while sitting on the white sand of a beach in Paunui, New Zealand. I remember the thought drifting into my head from the clear blue sky, "I will be a teacher." I have not changed lanes since.

To me there is still something distasteful about teaching; maybe it is acknowledging the fact that I must grow old while the students around me will be forever young. Maybe it is the lack of respect the public gives to the profession, or maybe it is the fear that I will look back in thirty years and see a long line of students who were completely unaffected by me being here.

John was a student who gave me hope that my purpose would be fulfilled through students like him. He seemed to need me. Mentally wrestling with me seemed to be the highlight of his day, and he relished being my shadow. I had given up on trying to dissuade him from visiting and had accepted my role.

One spring day, John came by to visit and told me he would be in my class next year. I had mixed emotions. I was accustomed to John in small doses and wondered if I could take him in ninety-minute spoonfuls. I was sure class discussions were going to be lively.

September arrived, and it was not long before John appeared at my door. His first sentence was a complaint about the summer reading for the class. He said it was all depressing. I told him that literature reflects life, and life is sometimes depressing. It wasn't until I knew John better that I realized John knew about suffering and depression far more than I did.

It didn't take long for the first class discussion to turn into a verbal fight. I remember asking what the class thought about *Grapes of Wrath*. Everyone loved the book, everyone except John. Soon the whole class had veins sticking out of their necks as they shouted down the infidel. John loved it; he even allowed a smile to cross his lips. He wanted to take them all on. One at a time they all took their shots, and John responded. The beauty of the entire argument was that they were thinking critically and were furious about literature. I needed to bring John into all of my classes to get the students riled up.

Discussions never went as planned with John's class. We might start out on the right track, but soon the students were livid about something John might say. He would get into heated discussions with people who agreed with him. He could not be agreed with or disagreed with; he had to be by himself fighting the world.

Everything John did was to elicit an angry response; he couldn't allow a day of rest for his classmates or for himself.

He wrote journals to draw me into his war of words, he gave speeches knowing how the class would react, he did everything he could to force his fellow students to see things from a different perspective. It was wonderful.

More than anything John wanted to be a writer, and he worked at the craft. He was constantly bringing me things to read that he had written. He didn't seem to understand English teachers already have plenty to read. I still found myself reading his work. His ideas were deep and mature. He was still a developing writer, but you could see him beginning to make great strides.

Then John started to miss school. I assumed that he had caught one of the many colds that circulate amongst the students and staff, but then I heard his father was dying. John's father had cancer and was in the late stages of the disease. Along with this news came the rumor that the family was going to lose their cranberry farm to foreclosure.

The early November weather in Southeastern Washington has a way of dampening your spirit, as well as the ground. The shorter days, wind and daily rain can turn the most optimistic person sour. The entire winter lies ahead, and you know that it is only going to get colder, windier, darker and wetter. On top of that, John had to deal with the impending death of his father and the loss of the family farm.

John arrived after school one day. He wanted to get his missed assignments. I talked to him for a little while, but avoided discussing anything personal. He looked thin and exhausted. There was something lost about him. There were too many late nights weighing heavily on him, and he was far too young to deal with everything life had tossed his way. If he were a heavyweight boxer, he would need to be given an eight count.

I couldn't help thinking about John the next few days and began to wonder if these recent blows would be enough to knock him down and out. His father's death seemed inevitable at the time, and John was still holding out hope for a miracle. Unfortunately a miracle wasn't going to happen. John's father died.

A week after his father's death John returned to school. He was still depressed and didn't spend as much energy trying to pick fights. His classmates reached out to him in friendship and comforted him in his time of need. These very same students, who earlier that year, could not look at John without spitting bile, were now bringing John into their group and allowing him to be one of the guys. Through the tragedy in his life, he had finally been accepted.

His healing process was long. Each day he seemed a little more like the old John and was soon stirring the pot again. Around Christmas time the school put up small evergreen trees for the different classes to decorate. It seemed a harmless tradition, but John was Jewish and couldn't let this tradition stand. He wrote a letter to the editor of the local paper about the "Christian tradition" of decorating trees. It was a scathing piece of work that upset many of the people in our school, including me. He was very proud of himself.

The last day before Christmas break, John wanted to talk about his letter and what I thought about it. Most often I would have avoided the conflict I knew John was setting up with me, but this time I took the bait and let him know what I really thought. We disagreed, but I stopped the discussion after ten minutes and gave a parting salvo about political correctness and baby-proofing the world before exiting the school and starting my Christmas break. As I walked out into the rain, John stood at the doorway with a smile on his face. He had accomplished his goal of engaging me in a heated discussion.

His death was mysterious, but at the same time seemed inevitable. Some people thought he might have committed suicide, but the John I knew would never have left this planet willingly without leaving a ten-page document designed to anger everyone he knew.

The first day back from break was difficult. I attempted to talk about John to his classmates, but found myself fighting overpowering emotions. I had to leave the room to compose myself. His incomplete life bothered me.

It didn't bother me that my final interaction with John was an argument. Our relationship was built on verbal sparring, and it seemed appropriate that it ended in that manner. In retrospect, our relationship was more than those little discussions, but those discussions defined a great deal about who John was.

I am still not sure how he died, but how he died is unimportant. In the end the number of people John impacted was extraordinary. I went to his funeral service and watched people share thoughts about John. He had done so much at such a young age. He had encouraged so many people and had been far more than a thorn in the side of those who knew him.

His incomplete life no longer bothered me, because his life was complete. He fulfilled his role here and helped me to define and come to solace with my own role as a teacher and a person.

The New Teacher

Forty-six kids. Forty-six kids in a classroom designed to hold thirty. It didn't matter that the kids were junior high-sized; junior high-sized kids made up for their lack of dimension with movement and odor.

No one in their right mind would ever put forty-six kids in a classroom and expect anything good to happen. If Sheryl had been an experienced teacher she would have known what was going on, but she wasn't. She looked at the class roster the day before school started and planned her innocent heart out. No one was looking over her shoulder to say, "Look, these kids aren't going to make it. Your job is to keep them contained. Don't send them to the office. Don't call home, because nobody there will speak English. Don't worry if they don't learn the language, because most of them will go back to Mexico in December and never return. These kids are here to pick our food and learn their place."

Sheryl didn't know any of this. She moved to California from Idaho because she heard there were teaching jobs, and when the Huron School District offered her a job, she took it because...well, because she had student loans to pay, she wanted to be a teacher since she was in fifth grade, the pay was thousands of dollars more than in Idaho, and it was in California.

The first day was a disaster. Four boys were sent to the office for refusing to take off their red bandannas, a fat little boy in the front row called her 'pendejo,' which was a new word for Sheryl, but sent the class into hysterics. A group of five girls in the corner of the room would not pay attention or go to the office when directed to do so. These kids might have only been living for twelve years, but they had already seen enough to know what the next fifty years looked like for them, and it didn't include sitting in some classroom writing papers for some gringa who would be gone in a year.

When Sheryl got back to her apartment that night she wanted to call her mom or dad and ask to come home, but her parents were divorced and doing their own thing, and their advice would probably be along the lines of "you should be happy to have a job in these tough times."

After some crying and a five-mile jog, she was ready to sit down and grade the student surveys she assigned. She remembered passing out the papers and telling the students, "These questions are about you. I want to know about you. So do your best and if there are questions you don't want to answer, you don't have to."

Of the forty-six kids, only about twenty of them bothered to answer all the questions. Ten of the surveys were returned without names and were covered with gang graffiti extolling the virtues of the El Norte gang. Most had a name and one-word answers on about half of the questions. A handful of students had done their best. Lupe said she wanted to be a nurse, Reynaldo wanted to be a Marine, Rebecca wanted to learn how to surf, Maria wanted to have five kids, and then there was Higinio.

Higinio didn't just answer the questions. He filled the page with words. Words that made Sheryl cry for the third time that day.

Question number one. What job do you want to do in the future? *I want to be a civil rights lawyer. I want a job where I help people. My family isn't rich enough to send me to college, so I need to work hard and learn so I can get a scholarship.*

Question number two. What is something I should know about your family? *My parents work in the fields. My momma and papa can't speak English, but my father tells me every night when he makes me do my homework that he works hard so I won't have to.*

Question number three. What is something you want to learn about this year? *I want to learn everything. I want to know why people are cruel. I want to know why there are borders between lands and people. I want to know why God put me here. I want to know about the stars. I want to learn about chemistry. I want to read stories about people in other places, and I want to be the best student you ever had. I know that isn't something I want to learn, but I don't want to be forgotten.*

Sheryl sat in her empty apartment trying to remember Higinio, to draw his face up into her mind, but she could not remember any of the students who sat quietly and did their work. The noisy, disrespectful students? She remembered all of them, their names, their faces, the sneers of disrespect, the posturing, and the anger pushed at her because they hated her.

The next day, as the forty-six students began piling into the classroom, she stood at the front of the class trying to pick Higinio out of the many brown faces. He was out there somewhere, but before the bell rang she had a situation on her hands. The same four boys came to class with their red bandanas hanging from their belt loops.

"Boys, please remove those bandanas before coming to class."

The largest boy, a boy twice the size of Sheryl, said, "We don't listen to you." The other boys stood waiting for her to respond. This was not a situation covered in the methods class of her small Christian liberal arts college, but she knew she could not lose this battle if she intended on winning the war.

"Put them away, or go to the office," she said with a strength that reached deep down inside her, down into the past, down to prehistory, down into the parts of her that were about protecting her brood. Her insides quivered and shook, but she stood firm and silent.

"Fuck you, bitch!" the big one said. "I'll go to the office before I disrespect la rasa." The four boys turned and walked out of the room slamming the heavy metal door as they left.

Sheryl got on the phone and called the office. "There are four boys who wouldn't put away their gang bandanas. I think they're coming to the office. They swore at me before leaving... No, I haven't called home... It just happened... Okay, I'll write a report when I have a chance... The biggest one swore at me... I'd prefer not to say... Okay, he said F U and then called me the word that rhymes with witch... Okay, thank you."

The entire incident lasted five minutes but it felt longer. She walked back to the front of the class and said, "Well, now. That was exciting. How about we get to taking attendance and starting class." She was looking forward to taking attendance because she could finally place a face on Higinio's name.

She mispronounced many of the names, but the students were used to that; the Huron School District had a history of hiring young, out of state, teachers with little experience, burning them out after one or two years, and hiring another fresh batch of cannon fodder.

When Sheryl came to Higinio, she was surprised; he was a small, shy, roly-poly kid. He raised his eyes from the notebook sitting on his desk when he heard his name, raised his hand, and looked up at his teacher in anticipation of being recognized. His eyes burned with hope.

"Hi, Higinio," she said. She smiled. He smiled back and melted Sheryl's heart.

The routines of the classroom continued for a few weeks. The four junior high gang bangers were each expelled one by one: two for fighting during lunch, one for throwing a stapler at Mr. Kanaterood, and the biggest one was sent to juvie for holding a gun to a kid's head in the restroom. Things that felt unacceptable in the first few days became standard operating procedure. Sheryl stopped calling home because it took so much time she never had time to grade papers and do everything else that was expected of new teachers. This job was not what she expected when she excitedly signed her name to teach in California, a place that had palm trees, warm weather, beaches, and blonde beach boys who swam in the waves. This was not the California of her mind, this was more Beirut than Berkley, but when she wanted to give up she would see Higinio's eyes burning with hope in the sea of faces. He was a candlelight in the storm of chaos.

The first day Higinio was absent Sheryl assumed that it was the late November flu that passed through her classroom like an Old Testament plague taking down three or four students at a time. After he was absent for three days, Sheryl asked one of the students she assumed was Higinio's friend where he was.

"He's working in the fields. His dad is sick and can't work."

"That's not right. That's illegal. A twelve-year-old child can't work in the fields," Sheryl said, as if she was angry at the student answering her question.

"I'm sorry, Miss. His family has to eat. It's how it is."

During her preparatory period, Sheryl tried calling Higinio's home, but the phone responded with a "The number you have dialed is no longer in service..." She hung up before hearing the entire recording. She marched over to the office, past the collection of kids waiting outside the principal's office and knocked on the door frame of the open door. "Mr. Apple, do you have a moment?"

Principal Apple turned away from the pile of work on his desk to see who was talking to him. "Sure, come in Miss Wilson. What can I help you with?"

Sheryl sat down in the one chair not covered in a stack of paperwork, "I have a student who is working in the fields instead of coming to class."

"Oh." Mr. Apple sat back in his chair. "Would you close the door?"

Sheryl stood up, closed the door, and sat back in the empty chair.

"I know you are a new teacher, and what I'm going to say is going to sound really cynical, but it's better to hear this now than to spend twenty years killing yourself."

Sheryl braced herself.

"This is a migrant school. These kids are here until their families move to the next place. Most of these kids are like leaves blown in the wind. We can't stop students from working in the fields because their families will just take them out of school, and we'll never see them again. If we don't say anything, they'll be back. It might not seem right, but that's the reality of it."

"But, the student I'm talking about is working because his father is sick. That's not right. Somebody needs to do something. He needs to be in a classroom, not in a field." Sheryl took a breath before saying the next thing. "Somebody has to care about these kids."

Mr. Apple sucked air through his teeth before saying anything. "I know you are upset, but calling someone, reporting this to someone, will only make more trouble for this family. There is a good chance they are here illegally. Notifying the authorities could get them deported. I'm not going to tell you not to do something you think is right, but please think about the whole situation before you do anything. You're a good teacher. You care. Sometimes caring makes people do things that end up causing more harm than help."

Sheryl nodded. "Thanks." Thanks was not what she meant, but it was what she said. She started crying by the time she was out of the office and spent the rest of her preparatory period trying to get herself together for the remainder of her classes.

That evening she could not sleep.

The next day Higinio showed up to class. Sheryl walked over to his desk, "I'm so glad you're here today."

He looked up at her and yawned. "Thanks, Miss."

"You look tired. Are you getting enough sleep?"

"Yes, Miss," he smiled. His tiny eyes had dimmed.

"Will you stay after class to talk with me?"

"Yes, Miss."

The class period was eternally long. Higinio put his head on the desk several times to sleep. When the end of the period arrived, Higinio walked to Sheryl's desk and handed her a salmon-colored paper.

"You're leaving?" Sheryl felt her eyes swell as she held the withdrawal form in her hand.

"Yes, my father is very sick. We need to go back to Mexico so he can get treatments."

"What's wrong with him?"

"The doctor says it's cancer," Higinio's bottom lip began trembling. Tears fell from his eyes.

"You should stay here. Your father should get treatments here."

Higinio shook his head. Tears fell onto his shirt, and his shoulders began shaking. "Please sign," he said pointing at the form.

"Oh, sweet pea." Sheryl stood up and hugged the little boy. He sobbed as she held his shaking body. "Oh, Higinio, I'm so sorry." Sheryl wanted to do something crazy, like take him home and run away from all the evil in the world, or call her parents and see if he could move to Idaho, but instead she stopped hugging the little boy, signed the salmon colored paper, wrote "Good Luck" in the box that said "Notes" and then watched Higinio walk out of her classroom never to return.

JON EEKHOFF

The Dining Room Table

Ours was not round.
Two boys on one side,
Two girls on the other.
A certain symmetry to
the arrangement.
An ordered family, or
the appearance of one?

We sat, ate, talked
and fought, side-by-side
always preserving the
appearance of order.
Never really orderly.
Never really side-by-side.
Never really anything
but a family.

Barry H Gets Busted

It was one of those nights. Winter had taken hold of the small college campus freezing everything solid and bringing on the darkness in the late afternoon. The basketball team recently returned from a long three-day road trip to Idaho, and we were tired, stiff and irritable. We had seen enough of each other, and tempers were sandpaper rough. It was the middle of another basketball season, and the end looked like a distant pinhole of light on a large black backdrop.

Our evening practice was reaching an end. We had been pushing one another physically and mentally for close to two hours. The fatigue of the road trip, lack of sleep, fifteen games and hundreds of hours of practice had piled on all of us like a heavy, damp, cold quilt. No one was comfortable.

Basketball teams, like marriages, go through highs and lows. The season starts with everyone fresh and hopeful. There is a common goal of winning and playing together. This blissful honeymoon period can last as long as the winning does. Two losses in a row can turn a happy marriage into a separation that leads to divorce. The dynamics of a college team are even more volatile, each player thinking he should be playing because most of them were The Man on their high school teams. They took all the big shots, they played the most minutes and were the coach's favorite player.

Once these guys join a college team, they start over, on the bottom. Early each season there is the hope that they will be an important player on the squad and will once again get the playing time and take the big shots. Halfway through the season most of the players are clawing at each other for playing time and recognition. Practices during these periods can be brutal.

Players literally scratch, bite and hit each other to move in front of whoever has "their spot." The players that are getting the game time respond by smothering and smashing the team members who are trying to steal "their spot." Practices keep the appearance of organized events, but they're really more like feeding time at the zoo. The biggest and strongest will survive, and the smaller and weaker will be relegated to the leftover scraps.

Over the length of a season, a player generally ends up hating almost everyone else on the team for a brief period. Some hatreds continue to build throughout the year until it becomes physical. Rarely do these conflicts end up looking like traditional fights with fists balled and punches thrown. That would be unteamlike. No, these fights are in the form of tossed elbows, knees being jammed into legs, knocking someone's legs from under them when they jump and excessively hard fouls. The goal of all this activity is not to injure a teammate, but to simply send a message, and that message is always understood by the team.

As this particular practice neared its end, we started conditioning drills where we were running the length of the court over and over again. The fatigue was building when I saw Juice dogging it.

Juice was a small, fast guard from Los Angeles. He was the kind of player who should always be in the lead in drills where speed is at a premium, but he very rarely was. He hung back, never giving his all, never pushing himself, always doing just enough to get by unnoticed. It made me furious. We moved to another conditioning drill where groups of guys would run taking turns on the court. Juice switched lines several times to avoid having to run when it was his turn. He walked over to the water jug behind one of the lines to get a drink. I moved up next to him and knocked the water out of his hand. "Get in line and run," I said. He cocked his head and began to form a response, but I cut him off. "Get in line and run like the rest of us, or I will flatten your ass." There was enough anger in my voice that he moved into line and took his turn. He avoided me for the rest of that drill.

Coach blew his whistle and called out the next drill, Gorilla Rebounding. This drill was probably the most intense and most physical of all. A shot would be thrown up by one of the coaches, and two teams of four players would scrap for it. Whoever got the ball would try to score the bucket. The first team to score five points got to take on the next team while the losing team ran laps. No one wanted to run, and no one wanted to lose. Just about anything was allowed; there was no reward for playing clean.

I gathered my usual group of guys. Todd M, a great shooter and jumper, Mark M, a dirty 6'8" player, and Steve M, our starting point guard and the scrappiest player on the team. We rarely lost Gorilla Rebounding, not because we were the most talented, but because we were not above cheating to win.

We started out against Juice's team. They usually provided little resistance; his team was a reflection of his personality, all flash and no substance.

The ball went up, we got it, scored it and tossed it back outside to the coach. After each bucket, the pressure ratcheted up a notch. A few of the players started to talk smack. Talking smack was a hidden skill. We never let the coaches hear us cuss out loud. We always acted like gentlemen. We sipped tea.

"You got nothing."

"Get ready to run."

"This board is ours."

The ball went up again; we rebounded and quickly scored the ball again. The shouts and wolfing began. "Game time! Get your sorry asses in gear! Start running!" Juice's team jogged off slowly with their heads lowered. They knew they had been beaten soundly and had nothing to say in response.

Barry H brought his team onto the floor. Barry was a senior and was a fantastic athlete. He had flashes of absolute beauty in his game that would cause the crowd to rise to their feet. He could also disappoint. One game he shot a ball over the backboard, all the way over the backboard, without touching anything. It was an amazing bit of miscalculation, and he was teased relentlessly about it. Barry, unlike the rest of the team, would just take the teasing and smile. He was too nice of a guy to play college basketball.

Barry could rise off the ground almost as if he never intended to return to earth. His leaping ability set him apart from most of us; we relied on position and physical play to get rebounds. Barry went up to meet the ball.

Joining Barry were Rod L, Daryl D and Jeff S. Rod was a nasty, intense player from New York. He was just over 6'2" with long arms and broad shoulders; he was an absolute animal during gorilla rebounding. I still have a scar on my arm from a deep scratch from Rod.

Daryl was an easy-going California native. His disproportionately long arms made him a terror against other guards in the league. His arms were normal for a 6'8" player, but Daryl stood 6'4". He was quick, thin and strong.

Jeff was the only white guy on Barry's team. He was a 6'9" goofy kid from Mesa, Washington, but he could play ball. If he got the ball near the hoop, you could count on the basket.

The two groups began positioning around the key, grabbing, pushing and playfully elbowing. Once the coach shot the ball, the playfulness ended. Rod got the best position and grabbed the first rebound. He tried to score the hoop and was instantly mauled by Mark M. Steve M brought both his arms down directly on Rod's bald head, sending him sprawling on the ground. Rod jumped up and moved quickly toward Mark, spitting bitterness as he closed in. Coach blew his whistle, stopping the action. A tone had been set; there would be no easy baskets.

The two teams fought for every rebound exhausting each other. The score stayed close. Each rebound, each basket increased the intensity. The two teams talked trash between each dead ball, but there was no humor in this talk. It was serious and angry.

Soon the teams stood tied at 4-4. The next bucket would win and send the other team to run. Everyone began grabbing and positioning as the ball went up. The ball bounded off the rim and was heading directly toward me. I held Rod down with my left arm and reached up with my right. I snatched the ball from the air and gathered myself for a shot attempt. I exploded toward the left side of the basket, and saw Barry getting ready to challenge the shot. My right arm instinctively shot out at him, planting an elbow somewhere on Barry's body. He instantly shrank away, and I laid the ball in with my left hand. "Stay down! Game time!" I shouted. My team began the trash talking as our opponents turned to run laps, everyone except Barry who was covering his face, laying on the ground.

I had no idea where I hit Barry with my elbow, but my elbow hurt. Looking at my pointy elbow I saw blood. I didn't know if it was my blood or Barry's. One of the assistant coaches bent over Barry to see what had happened and quickly turned away when Barry removed his hands. A pool of blood was forming on the ground by Barry's head.

I quickly cleaned my elbow and saw a gash oozing blood. The gash looked like two teeth marks.

The coaches were now getting Barry to his feet. Barry removed his hands, and I saw my handiwork. His mouth was a bloody mess. All four of his top front teeth were gone, his lip was cut cleanly through and blood was pouring out of the hole. My stomach turned. I walked away trying to gather my breath. I wanted to walk over to Barry, put my arm around his shoulder and tell him I was sorry, but that would have been out of character and soft. I needed to keep up appearances and put on a remorseless face.

Practice resumed, and Barry was taken away.

There is not a lonelier feeling than being injured badly. Your status has changed. You go from team member to hanger-on, an outsider, someone of little use. The team still welcomes you, but you are the one that feels out of place. It is a lost feeling, a sensation of uselessness. Many hours of rehabbing and conditioning lay ahead, and those hours will be filled on your own.

I suppose these injuries prepare you for the eventual reality of life after sports. Ex-athletes say they miss the camaraderie of the team more than they miss playing the sport. It is a reality that all athletes must face at some time; a small death along the trail of life is how a poet might describe these events. For an athlete it is simply a hole in their life that comes on suddenly and often without warning.

For those of us that were left behind, Barry was soon a distant memory. We finished practice, went to the cafeteria, showered and studied for class the next day.

Barry spent the subsequent three or four hours without teammates. He was taken to an emergency room for his lip and then to a dentist for hours of emergency dental repair. His senior season was now in jeopardy; there was a very real possibility that this injury might end his basketball career.

Barry didn't return to practice the following day, or the next day or the next. I began to wonder if the injury was worse than I imagined. My roommate Eddie was the first to see Barry. They had class together. Barry showed up with an enormous fat lip, lots of stitches and a broken jaw that was wired together. Eddie spent most of his description on Barry's lip. It was huge, the size of a fist.

Barry did not return to practice for more than a week. By then the lip had gone down, but it was still an ugly mess. The guys tried to make Barry feel at ease by giving him hell about his situation. Most of it centered on how he looked much better than he used to. Barry would nod and try to smile, but any movement of his mouth appeared to cause him pain.

Eventually Barry joined us in drills again, but he was tentative. He did not want to get injured. He managed to play four or five games to end his senior season, but he floated around the perimeter and showed nothing like his previous flashes of brilliance. His career ended quietly. Most seniors hold on to their dying careers and fight to continue. Barry simply bowed his head and jogged away. He was still too nice to play college basketball.

Lettuce

Lettuce is my life. Well, it is this summer. Why else would I be sitting in a TriGrow company van with a bunch of half-baked losers at 4:45 in the morning heading for Buttonwillow to look at a field of lettuce plants? To be honest, I guess I would just have to say that it is a job —a summer job. I am not hoping to become the West Coast expert on lettuce or any other crop; I am just the lucky guy that happened to be at the right place at the wrong time when the job opened. I don't know anyone who really likes to work, but you have to do something.

I may not love my job, but the farmers we work for love the job we do. For some reason, they believe we are competent and know what we are doing. If you have heard of the Peter Principle, then we are the agricultural wing of this theory. I couldn't spot a bad lettuce plant from a healthy one, but I still don the big white jumpsuit, grab a hoe and head into the field as if I have some idea about what I am doing. Most of the time, I look down the row and randomly pick a plant that looks weaker than the rest and hack it out. Darwin would be proud.

The faith the farmers have in us has really begun to surprise me because half the time that we show up our boss,

Don, is drunk off his butt, while the other half, he has a nice-sized hangover. The best days at work are the ones when Don had been up all night drinking Tanqueray and tonics. It's easy to tell when he'd been out all night because he keeps track of his drinks in a distinctive way: he takes the little red straw out of his drink, folds it into a triangle, stuffs one end of the straw into the opposite end, and does the same thing with every drink. After that he makes a little chain of red triangles. The days he shows up with a long chain are the best; it means we will do some light work in the morning, followed by a long break, followed by a long slow drive around the fields, followed by lunch, followed by a whole bunch of cribbage back at Don's house where we hide from his bosses. Then Don heads back to the Cotton Club's bar to start the routine all over again.

I'm often in a semi-coma watching the rows of grapes and cotton go by out of the corner of my eye. I do not know why I look. The San Joaquin Valley has yet to be featured on *Lifestyles of the Rich and Famous*; the tourist industry may be lagging behind the valley's real purpose, to put food on the table of the world. No one passes through the valley unless they have made a serious error in navigation: "Welcome to the driest, flattest, most boring place on earth" should be the valley motto.

The crew I work with is pretty much a bunch of blockheads. Chris is probably the smartest of the bunch because he made an attempt at being in the Navy before he dropped out of life and became a lettuce head. The other two guys, Phil and Ray, became lettuce heads straight out of high school, which puts them way down on the evolutionary scale in my book. I'm no Steven Hawking, but at least I can see that this job is not what I want to be doing when I am fifty. I am just putting in time trying to make some money so I can go back to Kings River Junior College and earn some more mediocre grades. I don't think Harvard's Law School is going to be offering me a full-ride any time soon.

On our way to the fields, the lettuce heads and me usually try to get some sleep. Nobody ever sleeps though 'cause driving on Highway 41 is like driving on the moon. I'm surprised a meteor hasn't hit anyone. The highway gets caked with sludge from all the farm vehicles driving from the mud roads that line the fields. The trucks pull onto the pavement with their muddy tires and leave a trail. When the mud dries out it is hard to tell the road from the dirt shoulder. It is not exactly the German Autobahn.

**

My attempt to sleep was cut short as Don slowed the van down and turned onto one of the dirt roads that led to our lettuce field. I started trying to use my psychic powers. "No work, no work, no work."

I don't think I have psychic powers, but it never hurts to try.

As we drove up to the field, Don was looking out the window at the lettuce plants, slowing the van to a creep.

Lettuce plants that are grown for seed don't look like the lettuce you see in the grocery store; they look like little lettuce Christmas trees and stand about six feet tall. Anyway, Don looking out the window was a sure sign that he didn't want to work; he was looking for a reason to take the day off. The lettuce heads and me were laying low in the seats acting like we were asleep so Don wouldn't feel any pressure from us. We didn't care to work, we got paid either way, and it's always more fun to sit in the van and play cards with the air conditioner on high than to look at lettuce plants in 110-degree heat. Don finally muttered something about it being too wet to work and stepped on the gas. This never failed to amaze me; how can a place that hasn't seen rain in over a month and has an average daytime temperature of 110 degrees be too wet? It wasn't a topic I would like to discuss at length with Don. If he wanted it to be wet, then it was wet. Maybe Don had some kind of Doppler radar and knew it would rain within the next three months and didn't want us to get caught out in a flash flood.

Don turned the van around and started back to the ranch headquarters. The lettuce heads and me were suddenly wide awake and talkative. Don pulled back out on Highway 41 and got the cruiser up to about 80 mph in 4.2 seconds. For some reason Don was under the impression that driving like a drunken sixteen-year-old would draw less attention, but he was the expert in this area, so I left the work-skipping options to him.

On non-work days we didn't go right back to the ranch headquarters, because the farmers were still in bed asleep. So Don usually drove around back roads at maximum speed while doing the morning crossword puzzle. When I say he did the crossword puzzle while driving, I mean he put the puzzle on the steering wheel and steered with his legs, looking out the windshield only when whoever was in the front passenger seat started to make squeaking noises and preparing for impact. This used to worry me, but I decided since Don was so used to driving drunk this technique was actually safer than being with him at night.

After we wasted enough time, Don headed for the ranch headquarters to meet with his bosses who got in around seven. Don usually went in and BS'ed with them, telling them lies about how hard we worked that morning.

Things were going to be different today though, 'cause Don suddenly slowed the van down and pulled a U-turn. The lettuce heads were looking at each other with panicked faces, and I felt a little queasy. I thought, "Are we going back to work?" Maybe Don's conscience finally got to him and told him, "All play and no work makes Don an unemployed guy."

That wasn't what was happening either. Don turned the van engine off and coasted to the side of the road. We parked right next to a watermelon field and inched toward a blue car parked next to the field. I recognized it as one of the security cars used to protect the watermelons. You see, the watermelons grown on this ranch were hybrids, and the farmers didn't want the field workers stealing the melons, taking them home and spitting seeds all over the yard. Next thing you knew the hybrid melons would be popping up all over the county and the farmers would be out mucho dinero. So they hired security guards to protect the fields from melon banditos.

As we inched closer to the car I realized what Don was up to. I could see that the security guy in the car was doing something he wasn't supposed to be doing: sleeping.

Don stopped the van and asked us if we could see if the guy was asleep. We all confirmed that he was either sleeping or had been shot dead by a watermelon bandito. Don opened his door quietly and snuck over to the security guy's door.

Don paused a second, processed the situation like a good manager would and then shouted like a loosed mental patient, "YOU'RE FIRED!!!" while slamming his hands down on the hood of the car.

The security guy's eyelids popped opened so wide I thought his eyes might fall out on the car floor. It is bad enough when you get woken from a deep sleep, but having to find your eyes on the floor of a dirty car just makes things more complicated. I know I would have been stunned if someone had yelled, "YOU'RE FIRED!" while I was dreaming about catching farm workers loading their trucks full of melons.

The security guy tried to say something, but Don turned around and walked as fast as his little alcoholic legs could carry him. The security guy was yelling something about he wasn't sleeping and how Don couldn't fire him. Don jumped in the van, cranked it on and floored it.

The tires screamed when we hit the asphalt road. Don was trying to break the land speed record for farm vans. We were bouncing down 41 as close to out of control as I ever want to be, with the van shaking so violently it felt like we were reentering earth's atmosphere from space. The lettuce heads said nothing, but kept looking at each other and making grunting pig noises, trying not to laugh.

Don was muttering something about that SOB security guard not doing his job, which was slightly ironic, since we were not doing ours at the time we caught him not doing his. The security guard was behind us, weaving down the road trying to keep up with our jet-powered farm van.

Don slowed down as we approached the ranch headquarters. It was nothing more than a dusty acre with a small brown rectangular manufactured home plopped down in the center, and two smaller buildings flanking it, along with a couple of gas pumps. With the speed of the van as he entered the lot, I thought it might be appropriate to have a parachute pop out the back doors, but it was too late for that. Don jumped out the exact moment the van came to a complete stop. It looked like he'd practiced this before, or maybe he was a stuntman in the winter or maybe this skill came in handy when running from the cops after being pulled over for drunk driving on the weekends.

Leaving the van running, he charged up to the headquarters, opened the front door and busted inside.

The lettuce heads exploded with laughter. They were all screaming about how big the security guy's eyes got and how mad Don was and how the security guy couldn't drive for crap. It was funny; I even started to laugh. Then the funniest thing happened- the security guy came motoring up to the compound at about 60 mph and slammed on the brakes, but instead of waiting for the car to come to a stop, he threw it into park while still going about 30 mph. The car stopped like it had hit a tree. The security guy's head bonked off the windshield and rebounded into the headrest. I think the windshield took most of the damage.

Don came blazing out of the office, moving somewhere between a race walk and jog, jumped back in the van and pulled around to the center of the office compound by the three large red gas pumps. He got out, unhooked the nozzle from the middle pump and started to fill the van up with super unleaded. This seemingly irrational behavior didn't surprise us at all. Nothing Don did surprised us anymore. I thought he must have been filling up the van to drive as far away from the security guy as we could. "If you cannot outrun 'em, drive till they run out of gas," must've been Don's strategy.

The security guy was yelling something at Don, and Don was yelling back. The lettuce heads were just eating the action up. I was getting a little scared. The security guy was just a little too upset and imbalanced about this whole thing. I always looked at getting fired as an opportunity for some needed vacation time; obviously the security guy was not a glass is half full kind of guy.

Don, still screaming at the security guy, opened the van door, took a piece of paper from the glove box and scribbled on it. Don shouted at the security guy that he was writing a note to the security guard's boss that he had been caught sleeping and was fired.

Don started toward the main office in an apparent attempt to drop the note off. The security guard charged towards Don. Don, not being the most nimble guy in the world, had second thoughts about charging into the office. Instead he sidestepped it back into the van and tried to close the door. I say tried to close the door because the security guy put his hand in the door right as Don was slamming it. The normal sound of a door slamming shut was interrupted by a dull, muted thud. The door popped open a little way and released the security guard's hand. He was hopping around the compound holding his hand and shouting stuff in Spanish. In times like these I wished I had paid more attention in my Spanish classes, though for some reason, I don't think they would have taught me any of the words this guy was yelling.

Don saw his chance to make a break for the office again. I was in the back of the van with the lettuce heads now, and we were all cheering Don on like he was running for the end zone in the Rose Bowl. The security guy must've heard us, 'cause he turned around and started after Don, to try and tackle him at the one. Both of them were approaching the door in slow motion, and Don never knew what hit him.

The security guard pulled out his 45, shouted something about not getting fired and then fired Don, right in the head. It wasn't like on TV. There was no huge thundering boom - just a crack and then some stuff flying out of Don's head. Don didn't fall and crawl around and die in anybody's arms. He just hit the ground like a slab of beef and didn't move.

The security guy looked down at Don, dropped his gun and fell onto the pavement crying.

I didn't know if I should play Dirty Harry, leap out of the van, dash over to the gun and hold it on the security guy; or if I should play me and cower on the floor of the van, worm my way up to the CB and call for help. I decided being me was best and crawled up to the CB and radioed for help.

When the cops finally showed, the security guy was still just sitting against the wall staring at the van. For a second I thought he'd fallen asleep again, but he hadn't. The cops took him away and the lettuce heads asked if I thought that we might still have jobs. I just looked at the dark pool of blood where Don died.

Escorting Emma

Walking an aisle in Walmart,
she slips her tiny hand into the crook of my arm.
Looking down on her, my little girl, I see
innocent round cheeks and blue eyes.

A pudgy four-year-old who loves pink
dresses and mommy's forbidden perfume.
I usher her through sporting goods
and hardware. We are quite a couple.

Me, well over six feet, hiding my gray hair
with daily beard trimming.
Her, three and a half feet of energy and
emotion. Full days of smiles and tears.

Glancing down, I am transported forward,
again I am escorting Emma down an aisle.
Her arm tucked tightly into mine.
Who will be waiting at the end of that Aisle?

Let her be forever four,
forever innocent,
forever soft,
forever mine.

Who will be the man to take her away?
Will he love her and protect her?
For now those questions shall remain.
I am content in this moment, escorting Emma.

Three Rivers

California Aqueduct

It wasn't really a river, rather it was a bend in the canal where a large oak tree grew shading the water from the hot San Joaquin summer sun, but it was a meeting place, a slight rise in a land so flat the farmers needed to hire men to tilt the land so the irrigation water would flow from one end to the other, and it had two escape routes in case the farmer who owned the land wondered what they were doing out there beneath that oak tree, but the farmer never came out there when they were swimming in the dank, warm water siphoned off from the California Aqueduct that split the valley from top to bottom; the farmer didn't care as long as they cleaned up after themselves, and they knew that was the deal, so they always packed the loose Coors Light beer cans in a sack or tossed them in the bed of the truck, but for their group this was the place, their little Eden in the middle of a scorching desert where there was never anything to do, so it became "the beach" because the real beach was still a three hour drive through winding roads and mountain, and they treated it like they treated Pismo, taking long beach towels, boom boxes with mixed tapes filled with Journey, Billy Squire, and AC/DC, and they brought plenty of liquid refreshments to keep the buzz buzzing in that low, dull place where the brain rested comfortably, where life and youth still blazed and burned brighter than the hottest place on the planet.

China Creek

On hot days, young people wearing cut-offs and flip flops climbed the smooth Phanerite stones bulging from the banks of China Creek looking for a spot to sun their already tanned bodies, some carrying Styrofoam boxes with ice, beer and wine coolers up the steep stones, while the experienced sun worshipers knew that cold cans of Budweiser and bottles of Bartles and Jaymes would remain chilly enough if kept in a backpack and then plunged in a back eddy of the river and experience also taught them that this was a river where one should not drink too much or act too boldly, since the *Sierra News* always had front page space for spring articles about drownings, usually young men from nearby military bases who didn't understand their fragile situation in the universe and thought they could swim across there or jump from that, only to find out too late that the core chilling cold of China Creek wasn't an abstract danger they could ignore while on leave, and the deadly mixture of youthful ignorance, testosterone, and alcohol cut away the too bold or the too drunk in a ritual that went all the way back to the beginning of time, when the granite rocks they climbed across were formed, when the water began tumbling toward the Pacific in a roar that never abated, through thousands of years, spilling over rolling boulders in a never ending cacophonous cascade of sound and gravity that traveled through time and space transporting waters from sky to land and back again, waters that might have touched Heraclitus's foot.

Wishkah

At low tide, the muddy banks of the Wishkah look like black tar heroin smoothed out by the thumb of God or black plastic stretched across the banks to prevent erosion and then forgotten about, so if the water were ever drained and a satellite picture taken it would look like a black snake with its tail twisting into the Olympic forests and its head stuck in Aberdeen, where on occasion you might find long-haired kids from around the world looking for the bridge that Curt Cobain slept under before rocketing to fame singing about teenage angst and anger, but when the tide rose the blackened banks disappeared under the slow flow of chocolate-colored water, covering the ugliness or beauty (depending on your perspective) of the slick sediment too thick for the current to carry out to the Pacific, the layers and layers of microscopic particles churned up by glaciers, or skimmed off by the rain storms upstream and then falling into some atomic-sized hole in the river bank to keep the water moving at its slackened pace, each little thing finding its place almost like it was premeditated, but more likely just a series of haphazard events leading to a conclusion never intended, an end to one thing and the beginning of something new, and that is the beauty of all waters and rivers, their beginning is their end, so it is up to you to decide if it begins in the sky or in the great oceans of the world, as it doesn't matter to the rivers whose job is to connect all things and bring them home.

Friday Afternoon Fever

We poured out of the dark cafeteria and into the clear sunlight of the playground. Another junior high school dance had passed; I still hadn't danced with Tammy.

I buttoned my Green Bay Packers jacket to the top and waited for the bus. My best friend, Bill, stood next to me with his blue nylon jacket zipped like mine, to the top. We were far from being the studs on campus, but we had our dreams, and mine was to dance with Tammy Neff. I think Bill's dream might have been for me to dance with Tammy, also.

When the bus came Bill and I got a seat near the front. Bill took the window because I had it yesterday, and we waited for the announcement that the bus driver made daily; we would be sitting three to a seat. Being on the bus waiting for someone to sit next to us was always a time of great excitement. Since Bill was sitting next to the window, he was hoping that an ugly girl would sit next to me, and since I was on the aisle, I was praying for a foxy chick. The wheel of fortune was spinning, and I could either be a lucky stud or a bankrupt pud.

It looked like pud for me today as the "Goodrich Blimp" was positioning herself for a landing on my seat. I left my leg daringly on the part of the seat she was about to land on, to discourage her from plopping down in my neighborhood. I quickly jerked my leg back home as I saw her huge butt making a rapid descent. If I didn't move fast, she'd turn my leg into a pancake. I imagined myself trying to explain to my mom why I was missing one of my legs when I got home and hearing her tell me that if I wouldn't have been playing those dumb games I would still have two legs.

I looked at Bill, and his grin was almost as big as the Blimp's butt, which made me feel a little worse, as if that were possible. I told Bill he had black stuff on his teeth even though he didn't, thinking that would shut his yap for a while.

The bus jerked to a start, and Bill whispered in my ear that I should put my arm around "my date." I told him I would, but I didn't think my arm would reach around her. Bill started to laugh, but closed his mouth quickly so no one would see his black teeth.

As we neared my drop-off point, I looked down at my leg next to the Blimp's. Her thigh made my leg look like a broom handle. I started to wonder if all the fat on her leg could suddenly turn to liquid fat, float through my jeans by way of osmosis, and end up on my leg. I could see myself getting off the bus with one super fat, jiggly leg and one normal-sized one and trying to walk. Everyone on the bus would laugh as I wobbled down the street with a fat leg and a skinny one. When the bus finally stopped, I squeezed out of my seat and hopped off. Just to make sure, I looked down at my legs to check that they were both the same size as when I got on the bus. They were. I walked home thinking about Tammy and how she would be mine soon.

Tammy was in my English class. She sat right in front of me, and on good days she would even pass papers back to me. Not that she ever looked back, but she knew I was there, 'cause she had to be handing those papers back to somebody.

I don't know if it was her long blonde hair that would fall on my desk as she fluffed it up with her fingers or the flowery smell that she always had as I passed by her to sharpen a pencil or turn in work, but there was something about her that just drove me crazy. The best thing about her was that no eighth-grade guys were after her; most of the good-looking seventh grade girls had been snatched up already. I knew that my luck might run out if I didn't act soon.

The weeks before the next dance passed quickly, and I thought out all the ways I could ask Tammy to dance. I settled on, "Do you want to dance?" I also decided that if I acted cool and had just a little deeper voice it would be much more effective. So, I practiced in front of the mirror for hours saying it over and over again in my new cool deep voice. When I tried practicing my new voice around the house my mom took my temperature, and my little sister said I was being weird. I took these as good signs.

The final touches to my boogie down plan were moving forward. Next on the list was clothing. Light-blue, flare-legged Toughskins may get you through elementary school, but what I needed was something that screamed, "far out." Angel Flight slacks. They were the kind of pants John Travolta wore in *Saturday Night Fever.* If I had those on I would be noticed.

The next time my mom took my sister and me to the mall, I made a bee line for Miller's Outpost and there they were: two racks of Angel Flight slacks. I hurried over to the rack with the tan colors and searched for my size. A pair of champagne (not tan) pants marked 28x32 vaulted out, and I grabbed them then headed for the changing corral.

Once there, I jerked my pants down and slid them over my tennis shoes. One of the greatest benefits of bell bottoms was never having to take your shoes off when changing. I grabbed the polyester slacks, slipped them quickly over my shoes and zipped up. Standing in front of the full-length mirror was one groovy-looking dude. Whoever said, "Clothes don't make a man," never put on a pair of Angel Flight slacks.

Now came the most important part. I did a few poses like John Travolta: right hand pointing up, left hand on the hip. It worked, I looked great, and my dream was going to come true. Out of the corner of my eye, I saw the price tag dangling from a belt loop during one of my more expressive poses. I grabbed the price tag and turned it over. It read $40.00.

Tears welled up in my eyes; my mom would never buy these for $40. Just this year, she bought me football cleats for $9.99, saying, "I'm not going to spend twenty dollars to watch you sit on the bench!" She always knew how to say the right thing.

The pants might as well have said one billion dollars. It was the same thing. I slowly slid the pants back off and crumpled them against my face. My tears streamed into the finest polyester fabric known to man. I breathed deeply and tried to get control of myself. I pictured myself trying to ask Tammy to dance in Toughskins; it was not a pretty picture. I wanted her to see the really groovy dude that I was, but in Toughskins it was an impossible task.

I did my best to hang the slacks back on the hanger, but for some reason my hands were retarded when it came to putting stuff on hangers. I took a good look at myself in the mirror to see if it looked like I had been crying and decided it didn't. I opened the corral door, and there stood my mom and sister. I knew my mom would ask about the slacks, and I knew what would happen when I told her the price, but I tried anyway. My mom flinched, kind of like when you have a dream about somebody throwing a ball at you. She looked at my bloodshot eyes, paused and asked if I had seen the Super-Bells that were on sale.

Ten minutes later, I was the proud owner of a pair of Levi Super-Bells, the biggest bells made. That certainly helped soften the loss of the Angel Flight slacks, but I would need to be twice as cool in Levis.

The day of the dance arrived, and I got up ready to ravish the women of the world. I bathed for a second day in a row, a rarity, and even washed my hair like the instructions on the bottle tell you to. Wash, rinse and wash again. I splashed on my dad's Old Spice and brushed my teeth till my gums bled. The final touch was my green mesh Kawasaki shirt, and my new Super-Bells, unwashed so that they would be a stunning blue and not faded.

After ignoring the stupid things my little sister said at the breakfast table I made my way out the door and towards my bus stop. Bill met me outside and immediately noticed my pants. He said that they looked a little stiff and wanted to know if they had been washed. I lied and told him that they had been washed, but I took them out of the dryer before they were completely dry, which I thought was a pretty good lie considering my time limitations.

I wasn't so sure if my grand plan of wearing unwashed pants was so wise now. I did notice that they rubbed on my thighs a little more than my other pants, and they looked a lot like that cardboard robot outfit I had to wear for the elementary Christmas pageant.

Bill and I got to the bus stop.

Trey Street, an eighth grader, was the next to ask me about my pants, and I stuck to the company line, washed but not dried totally. Trey then struck up a conversation with Bill, which I thought was kind of weird because Trey hadn't really talked to either of us about anything since fourth grade. It didn't take long for me to figure out why though. Harold Steele was sneaking up behind Bill with a lighter and was about to light Bill's hair on fire. I was caught between my loyalty to Bill and my wanting to be in the in-crowd, so I said nothing. Harold moved the lit lighter closer and closer to Bill's dirty blonde hair until smoke started to rise, and then small flames drifted up the back of Bill's head. Harold immediately started swatting Bill's head, which came as quite a surprise to Bill, since he was involved in a deep discussion with Trey. Harold violently beat Bill until the flames were all out, at which time the surrounding bus stop crowd broke out in laughter. Bill laughed too, but I knew he felt like an idiot. He took out his brush and tried to comb his hair, but it was a big glued-together mess. The worst part was the smell; burnt hair has one of the most distinct smelly smells.

Bill was okay and seemed to handle the whole situation very well, even the part where I watched the whole thing. When we got on the bus, Bill's hair was the topic of conversation with everyone but me and Bill. It was hard to ignore the smell, but we had business to tend to. Bill and I plotted strategy on the way to school hoping to find that final angle that would put me on top of all the rest of the idiots that asked Tammy to dance. I had to do it, I could wait no longer for fate to put us together, and I had to act on my own.

Bill and I decided that I should wait for the last song since it was always a slow one and that would give her a chance to be next to me for a while and see just how much she was going to like it. By waiting for the last dance she would also have the memory of dancing with me for much longer. And it would give her something to giggle about with her friends after we had been going out for a couple of years.

When it was time for the dance the entire school piled into the cafeteria along with one very nervous and sore person, me. The insides of my thighs had been rubbed raw by my pants, and I could only walk stiff leggedly and slowly. I guess I looked like a seventh-grade version of the Frankenstein monster.

Bill was no help, asking me this and asking me that, getting me into a state of nervousness only experienced by people about to be put in the electric chair. The songs seemed to drone on and on. I played the scene over and over in my mind. Walk up, pose, present my hand to Tammy, pull her to her feet and ask seductively, "Care to dance baby?" We would then spin across the floor together as the disco beat drove us to boogie ecstasy. The whole school would step back and clear the floor. When I finally snapped back to reality, I realized the dance was almost over.

Fly, Robin, Fly was the last fast song before the final slow song would begin. I started to make my way over to Tammy. Slowly, stiffly I shuffled so I could get the last dance with her. My hands started to sweat; the milligram of confidence I had built up to this point was now gone. *Fly, Robin, Fly*, was winding down as I approached Tammy. I caught her eye, and my heart jumped a beat. I walked within talking distance and began to open my mouth. She looked at me, waiting for me to speak. I looked at her waiting for something to come out of my mouth, but nothing would. I sounded like I had something caught in my throat that prohibited me from talking. Finally, I got out a raspy syllable of a word; I think it sounded something like, "Huhhhnn."

She said, "What?" and her friends started laughing like I just told the funniest joke ever told. But not Tammy. She waited for me to gather myself and finally ask, "Would you dance with me?" It felt as though a great weight had been lifted off my shoulders, and I held my sweat-covered quivering hand out to her.

Tammy smiled sweetly and said, "No."

My heart was crushed. I said, "Thanks." I wasn't all that thankful, so I don't know why I said that. I turned towards the crowd of boys; I could see Bill looking at me as I tramped back to the darkness of our seats. My thighs didn't hurt anymore. Nothing hurt anymore. I was numb.

When I arrived back at my seat Bill asked why I wasn't out there dancing with Tammy. I told him that she simply wanted to rest and not dance. Just as I finished my sentence, I looked up and there was Tammy, out on the dance floor, with Mr. Popular. He was already in eighth grade and crushed me through football, basketball, and girls.

I'm sure Bill saw them too, but he didn't say anything. I buttoned my jacket to the top and walked towards the door, tears welling up in my eyes. I could hear Peter Kris singing *Beth* as I opened the door of the cafeteria and walked out into the bright playground.

Max Miracle Boy

A heavy door had slammed releasing
Max's fingertip from his tiny hand.
His lonely finger was found lying cold,
on smooth cement, placed in a plastic
urn and whisked, with Max, to safety.
Doctors reunited Max, made him whole.

Two Sundays passed before Max rematerialized,
right arm in a sling, finger wrapped in gauze.
The lone white digit enlarged by cruel fate.
This quiet boy drew my brief attention.
Beneath white fabric a miracle waited.
A fingertip fused by a doctor's hand
was now growing together by an unseen hand.

A month passed, Max was in church unbound,
all ten of his digits now on display.
The finger remained swollen and shortened, a token,
the price of this small miracle paid in full.
A blank space remained where once rested a nail;
an unnatural wrinkle ringed his blunt fingertip.
Was the nail drawn beneath the blemish
and buried deep below his smooth skin?

Talkin' Trash

"That's a bullshit call," JB yelled at Darryl.

"Ball! My ball, my call," Darryl shouted back as he moved toward the top of the key.

"It's a bullshit call."

"Fuck you, JB. You got your hands all over me every time I go to the hole. I could call a foul every time."

"You do. You got a pussy call every time. Everybody here knows it. Game gets tight, Darryl's gonna make a bullshit, pussy call. Here's the ball, pussy," JB said tossing the basketball against Darryl's feet.

The ball ricocheted off Darryl and skidded across the floor toward the players waiting for the next game.

"Get the ball bitch," Darryl shouted to JB. One of the waiting players scooped up the ball and passed it back onto the floor. "Ten, nine," Darryl announced to the teams on the court.

"Ten, ten," JB corrected. "It's ten, ten, bitch. I know you can't fuckin' add, but it's ten, ten," JB picked up the ball, tossed high into the air forcing Darryl to raise his arms to catch it. With the ball above Darryl's head, JB moved in tight to Darryl's body hoping to force a quick turnover.

"Back off, bitch," Darryl spat, ripping his elbows close to JB's face and into triple-threat. Darryl's teammates jammed their bodies against their defenders, and Howie popped from the pack free from his defender. Howie curled his cut as he approached the three-point line, turning his body so Darryl could hit him with a sharp pass. Darryl stepped through JB's arms and extended. Flicking his wrists he snapped a flat pass into Howie's shot pocket.

Howie hopped to set his feet, coiled, and then sprung into the air. The defender closing out on his shot got a hand up, but Howie only saw the hoop. He never saw anything else when he shot, just the hoop. The ball floated off his fingers, rotated three times and splashed into the net.

"Game!" Darryl shouted. "Sit down, bitch!" he spat at JB.

Howie's teammates slapped hands, "Nice shot," they each said.

JB stood at the top of the key, hands on his hips, "FFFUUUUUCCCCKKKK! Another bullshit call. Every game! Every fuckin' game. Bullshit calls D. Bullshit calls."

"Hey, JB," Darryl said dribbling the ball out from beneath the hoop, "Go sit down bitch!"

"Fuck you, Darryl. That was a bullshit call, and you know it. Little bitch." JB started walking toward the sideline, "Whose got next? You need one?"

"I'm next, JB, but we got five," Kevin said.

"Fuck!" JB shouted again, snatching up his t-shirt. "I ain't gonna wait two games. All because of pussy Darryl and his bullshit calls."

"Hey, JB," Darryl shouted from the top of the key as the new teams organized themselves for the next game. "You're a fouling bitch, but you didn't touch me that time."

JB tossed his balled-up t-shirt against the bleachers and stomped toward Darryl. Darryl dropped the ball, turned, closed his hands, and shifted his weight back. As JB moved into range, he shifted his weight forward and twisted his body. It was a quick, sharp strike that glanced off JB's left cheekbone. JB hadn't seen the punch coming and fell to the ground face first.

"What now bitch!' Darryl screamed, dancing around the dazed JB. "What now!" Teammates pulled Darryl away, but Darryl continued shouting at JB with his arms raised above his head. "Who's a bitch now!"

JB gathered himself and stood. He wobbled, "I'm ready now. Let's go! Come on, bitch! I'll fuck you up."

Darryl worked free of his teammates and moved toward JB, but the team intervened pulling both players away from each other. "JB, you need to go to the trainer," Kevin said moving JB toward the exit. "Come on, I'll take you there."

JB pushed forward, away from Kevin and walked down the stairway toward the training room. His mind was still a jumble of mixed thoughts, and he moved like a drunk down the hallway. A large welt formed beneath his left eye, and he could feel it swelling.

Twenty minutes of icing reduced the mouse, but JB's mind still hadn't cleared. He could not remember the punch, he did not remember standing afterward and challenging Darryl. He felt drunk, as if his brain were underwater or just out of reach. The next few days he had terrible headaches, but told no one. He laughed about the punch, but when he was alone, it terrified him.

The Inheritance

Each morning, before leaving for third grade, James combed his hair over his forehead to cover the four-inch scar sitting above his left eye like an angry caterpillar. It reminded both he and his father about what could happen when dad drank too much. They never talked about the scar. They never talked about the drinking, and they never talked about why his father didn't take the six-year old boy to the ER after the bleeding wouldn't stop, and three towels were soaked in blood. James hadn't agreed to ignore the scar; it was just one of those things.

An empty stomach was the only alarm clock James needed. The cold morning air filled the tiny trailer as James foraged through the small kitchen. He opened all six of the cabinets never making a sound, like a mouse looking for something left behind. Some mornings he left the trailer and climbed through the woods to the bus stop with an empty stomach, but on this morning he found a loaf of Wonder bread in the third cabinet. He reached for the bread, extending as far as his fragile body would allow, grasped the plastic bag and pulled it down. James stepped lightly over the uneven linoleum floor to the toaster and slipped two slices of the bread into the slots. He pushed the plastic lever down and held his tiny hands above the toaster to catch the escaping warm air. When the bread popped up, he gathered it in and held the slices between his hands until all the heat passed out of the toast.

The warm bites filled James with euphoric pain. He considered toasting two more slices, but he knew every slice of bread, every Bud Light, every can of chili had a price, so he tucked his warm hands into his grimy jeans and headed out into the damp December morning.

He kicked through the dead leaves as the grey morning piled itself onto his narrow shoulders. Tiny, misty breaths escaped his mouth as he climbed toward the bus stop without the slightest thought of the crushing weight of everything.

He knew the empty bus would arrive soon. He would find his seat, the one above the heater, and hang his cold feet in the stream of warm air escaping from the metal box. On very cold mornings, Jayne, the bus driver, would let James lay on the floor in front of the heater until she picked up the Anderson kids. He would press the palms of his hands against the mouth of the heater and let the blowing air fill the sleeves of his tattered sweatshirt.

Once the cold of the world slid away, James would pull his hands back, tuck them under his armpits, pull his knees up, and fall asleep to the rolling motion of the bus.

Jayne tried to keep him awake by talking to him on the PA system. "Wiggle your foot, James. Are you awake, sweetie?"

He would thrust his foot into the aisle where Jayne could see it moving.

"Thanks, sweetie." When they approached the stop to pick up the Anderson kids, James knew to crawl into the seat and sit up.

The school day was parceled out in painful chunks, each one seemingly designed to remind James of the things he couldn't do. His mysterious handwriting, messy desk, plodding oral reading, and powerlessness to recall basic math facts challenged the most talented teachers at Meadow Lake Elementary.

No one teased James to his face anymore, not after what happened to Bobby O'Reilly on the playground. Bobby was a big fourth grader, much bigger than James, but they lived in different worlds. Bobby's Catholic upbringing of sin and forgiveness had not prepared him for James' unforgiving rage.

Bobby used the singsong voice of the playground to hurl his insult. "Hey, Booger Hands, take a bath. Take a bath."

"Say it again, and I'll kick your ass," James shouted strutting toward the larger boy.

"Booger Hands."

"Say it again."

"Booger Hands." Bobby tried to run, but James grabbed him by his red winter coat and did not let go, an ant attacking a flapping butterfly.

Bobby tried to maintain his dignity as James pulled him to the ground and beat him. Bobby did not realize how real it all was until it was too late. This was not pretend. This was not playground. This was primal, a beautiful savagery. James created his masterpiece with precise blows to the kidneys, punches to the neck, and pointed elbows to Bobby's unprepared body.

Bobby felt real pain for the first time in his life. He had never been hungry. He had never been cast aside like the world's trash. James unlocked a door to a world Bobby did not know existed. This was James' world.

So when James straddled Bobby's limp body and continued punching his broken face, he felt the warmth and power of his inherited gift, his gift for cutting into the flesh of the world and letting the guts of comfort and safety spill out onto the street.

The recess monitor blew her whistle. A little whistle was not going to stop James from extracting what he could from Bobby. The fight lasted one minute, but one minute was enough time for a boy with James' experience. When it was over, the kids who cheered for a fight had been given more than they knew was available from this world; they wanted playground violence not blood. James grabbed the dark curtain and pulled it back: the curtain to a world where people bled from their ears and were driven away in an ambulance.

His father scolded James as they sat in the office at Meadow Lake Elementary and said, "I raised him to know better than that." All the adults nodded solemnly and sent James home for a week.

The cold walk across the parking lot to the truck that smelled of stale Bud Light and wintergreen-chewing tobacco was silent. James played the role of regretful purveyor of violence. He climbed into the rusty truck, pulled the seatbelt across his waist, and looked toward his father.

"Well," his father said, "looks like you got some free time on your hands." Reaching over, he tousled his son's uneven hair and smiled. "That's my boy."

Old Growth

The Evergreens here are stunted
By seawater seeping up during high tide.
Without constant rain these green branches
Would brown and drop.
Their great taproot searches for an Artesian well
Flowing below the sandy soil.

My stunted heart beats with the everyday
But has not found the eternal source.
Reaching out into the unknown
Beyond blood,
Beyond the pulse of the world
Is the mysterious realm.
A place where wind and warm rays don't exist.

Each Sunday I look out these church windows
Hoping to see a great Cedar rising
Above the rest. Bending toward the Sun,
Reaching for the heavens,
Growing stronger, taller for some unknown
Reason.

The $92 Donut

What does a $92 donut taste like? Well, it tastes good, but when buying a $92 donut I have a few suggestions:

1. Park your car where you can see it.
2. Read all the signs where you park your car.
3. Know that Portland is Weird and therefore probably has weird laws.
4. Don't allow a $92 donut the power to spoil your day, bite its head off and eat it.

The donut is from Portland's too famous Voodoo donuts, and it has a retail price of $2, but if you park your car where I parked, the total price of visiting Voodoo donuts is $92, once you add in your $90 parking ticket.

How does one become the beneficiary of a $90 parking ticket? This is an excellent question, and one that I will try to answer. Mistakes are always easier to analyze in retrospect so after a few days to examine the situation I think I have put together enough excuses to make it sound like I have been victimized. This is an important step for all outlaws like myself.

Mistake number 1: I live in a town where parallel parking is a skill that is rarely used. Can I parallel park? Yes! Well, kind of. Okay, I can when I really have to, but when I see an open space that does not require parallel parking, I take that one instead of shimmying into a pair of pants that no longer fit. So, when looking for a parking spot in downtown Portland I passed up a perfectly good space so that I could park in one of the three open spots at the end of the street.

Mistake number 2: Ignorance. I am ignorant about many things in the world: String Theory, the life cycle of Voles, Advanced Math, and laws related to parking in Portland. Did you know that there are parking spaces for Carpool Vehicles? Well, there are. What is a carpool vehicle? You got me on this one. I think there are vans that are white and carry Portlanders who don't want to ride bikes but still want to be self-righteous. Does that mean that a car driven from Washington State carrying enough people to drive in the carpool lane can park there? Obviously not. Why not? Because a car with Washington license plates is an easy way to make ninety bucks for the city of Portland.

Mistake number 3: Even if you pay for parking, have a parking spot, and there is no indication on the parking space that it is reserved for Carpool Vehicles, you can still end up with a $90 parking ticket. I suppose this is the most annoying aspect of the whole thing. I paid to park AND got a ticket. So, for those Math majors out there, you can add $1 for a total of

$93, but only twenty-five cents of that dollar came from my pocket since my friend paid seventy-five cents of the parking. He also gave me $45 to pay for his half of the ticket, so what started as a simple math problem has now turned into a Common Core word problem because he also bought a donut, but I paid for it to save time. So, if you were a third-grade student you would have to write the problem out and explain it using your words. Here is how I would answer this problem when I was in third grade: "$90 is a lot of money. Donuts should not cost that much."

Mistake number 4: Read all the signs on a street before parking. Yes, that even means reading signs that are several parking spaces away at the end of the block. Sometimes cities try to save money (aka, screw tourists) by reducing their signage and environmentally friendly cities might even try to save the salmon by not painting curbs blue, or white, or orange, or red, or pink to indicate special parking situations. This salmon thing is out of control in the PNW. First it was the dams, then it was "Don't dump pesticides in the river," and now I have a $90 parking ticket. Just to get even, I am going to kill and eat a salmon this summer.

After I took the ticket from my window, it took me a good five minutes to figure out that I was parked in a restricted spot. Only then did I see the little sign at the end of the block with some nonsense about reserved for carpool vehicles. The irony that I was traveling to Portland to buy books, and I did not read the important words on the sign has not been lost on me. (Irony is much better when it relates to someone else.)

Mistake number 5: Wanting to eat a donut. There is no excuse but this particular donut has a big slab of bacon. You must admit (even you vegans) that bacon is awesome, and putting a full piece of bacon on a maple bar is one of mankind's greatest inventions. Since I was hungry, I probably did not take enough time to find a parking space. Is this a crime? Apparently, it is.

Northwest Exposure

The sound of a small engine revving woke Paul. He kicked his legs out of bed and sat up. "Annie, do you hear that?"

"Huh?" Annie lifted her head off the pillow.

"Listen," Paul said. The dim light of morning filled the small cabin as they waited. There was a faint sound, like a chainsaw, or maybe even a few chainsaws coming from the south. Paul stood up, pulled on his flannel shirt, and walked to the front door.

The familiar wall of trees outside the cabin blocked his view, but the sound was certainly chainsaws, the small engines revving and pausing like bees caught in a jar.

Then he heard a crack. He knew the sound, the sound of the heart of a tree breaking, followed by the whoosh of the tree falling with a soft thud. He raced back to bed, slipped into his jeans, laced his boots, and grabbed his heavy jacket. "Stay here. It sounds like somebody's cutting our woods."

"Daddy," a small voice called from the loft.

"It's okay, Emma. Come down and get in bed with mom. I'll be right back."

"Be careful," Annie called to him as he left.

Once outside, the noise increased. It was coming from the family homestead, the two hundred acres Paul's great grandfather claimed on the northern portion of the Olympic Peninsula nearly a hundred years ago. He trudged down the worn trail toward the sound, his breath smoking in puffs before him in the early October morning.

He heard another crack and whoosh. Paul ran toward the sounds. When he finally saw what he'd been hearing, his heart jumped.

There were three or four men with large chainsaws, orange safety vests, and orange hardhats moving around the hillside. Four heavy logging machines were parked on a freshly cut dirt road near the top of the rise, watching, like the faces on Mount Rushmore.

Paul stepped toward the widening clearing. He waved his arms frantically as he approached, shouting. No one heard him, but he waited until one of the chainsaw operators saw him. The logger hit the kill switch on the saw, grabbed a walkie-talkie and raised it to his mouth. Within a few moments all the noise and activity stopped, and Paul walked into the clearing toward the nearest logger.

"Hey!" Paul shouted. "This is my family's property. What're you guys doing here? You're in the wrong place."

The logger pulled off his headphones and looked at Paul, "What?"

"This is my family's property. You guys are logging the wrong spot." Paul looked around the clearing. Ten trees were already down.

"Nope, this is the right spot," the logger said. "There's a guy who comes in and marks all them trees. He uses GPS. It's accurate."

"Well, it's not accurate this time. This is my family's land. We've owned it for a hundred years."

"Check with the foreman," the logger said, pointing up the hill. "Dude in the silver hardhat."

Paul looked up the hillside, saw the silver hardhat, and started walking. The foreman stood watching Paul move through the graveyard of freshly cut trees.

As Paul got close he shouted to the foreman, "You guys are cutting my trees. This is my family land."

"We can look at the map if you want, but we measured it yesterday with GPS," the foreman said confidently.

"Yeah, let's look at a map," Paul said nearly out of breath.

"Okay, you own all this land?" the foreman asked.

"My family does. I own that chunk up there. This plot's my cousin's."

The two men walked toward a large white truck parked on the ridge. "Your cousin live in Portland?"

"Yeah."

"Last name's Cook?"

"Yeah."

"Well, we're harvesting these trees for a guy in Portland named Cook."

"He'd never do that. He agreed to never log this."

"You seen timber prices lately?"

"No."

"You should take a look. First and second growth timber is at an all-time high." The foreman arrived at the truck, opened the driver's door and reached into the cab. "Here's the map. Let's take a look."

He unfolded the map on the hood of the truck and showed Paul the forty-acre box outlined in red. "This is the chunk of land we're contracted to log."

Paul looked at the map. "Shit."

"So, we okay?"

"I guess. I can't believe he'd sell."

"You seen timber prices?"

Paul stood stunned for a moment. "How do you know which trees are on the line here?" Paul pointed at the red line separating his property from his cousins.

"All the trees we're cutting have a red X spray painted on them. Most of the trees on the property line we leave."

"Good."

"There is one big cedar in the back corner we decided was mostly on this property, so we are going to harvest it. We could toss a couple hundred bucks your way for the 10% that's on your property."

"The big cedar?" Paul pointed back toward his cabin.

"Yeah, it's back in this corner." He pointed at the line on the map.

"You're cutting all the way back to there? That's my property," Paul poked the map forcefully. "That really big cedar is mine. My daughter has her swing on that tree."

"According to the GPS..."

"Your GPS can kiss my ass! That tree isn't coming down! That tree is mine! Don't touch that tree or you're going to have every government agency I can call crawling all over this lot."

"Maybe you should call your cousin. He can decide whether to keep it or not."

"He isn't deciding anything. Don't touch that tree."

"Call your cousin."

"Don't touch that tree," Paul shouted at the foreman as he turned and stomped back home.

When Paul got back to the cabin, he tried calling his cousin, but no one answered. Paul left three voice mail messages before giving up.

That evening he sat on the porch with his wife and daughter listening to the buzz of greed coming from his cousin's property.

"Why are they doing that, Daddy?" Emma asked.

"I don't really know, Em."

"Did they kill the baby woodpecker?"

"What? What baby woodpecker, Em?"

"We found a dead baby woodpecker on the porch this afternoon," Annie said.

"Oh, maybe, Emma. There are probably lots of birds who are losing their homes down there."

"That's sad, Daddy. That makes me sad."

"Me too, honey," Paul said picking Emma up and holding her on his lap.

The porch Paul's family sat on was made from the logs that once stood on this spot. He wasn't some hippie-tree-hugger opposed to cutting timber; he cleared the two acres on the hilltop for a garden, he burned wood to heat his cabin, he could handle a chainsaw, he knew how to cut a wedge in a tree to make it fall right where it ought to, but he would never sell wood to a mill so it could be turned into a house in Japan.

When twilight passed over the hillside and all the noise of the day faded into the woods, Paul guided his family down the trail to see what was left of his cousin's lot.

Through the dying light, they could see how much progress the loggers made that day. Three large slash piles dotted the center of the scarred land like buttons on a vest of destruction. Fresh stumps oozed sticky sap, a stack of clean logs rested on a pile near the top of the hill. Four hulking pieces of yellow heavy equipment sat parked on the new rust-colored road gashed into the hillside.

"I can't stand to look at it," Annie said as she put an arm around Paul's waist. "I'm going back to the cabin."

"Take Emma with you. I'm gonna look around."

"Okay, come on sweet pea, let's go back to the cabin and make dinner."

"I wanna swing," Emma said.

"Not today sweetie. Maybe tomorrow all these men will be gone, and you can swing then."

"Daddy?"

"Yes, Em."

"Why are they doing this?"

"Money, Em. They do it for money."

"Can't you just give them some?"

"I wish it was that easy. Go with mommy. I'll be up in a minute.'

Paul walked up to the machines to have a look. It was unlikely the keys would be left but Paul looked anyway. He checked to see if the gas caps were locked; they were. He crawled over the two Cats, one for brush and one for roads, and found nothing interesting. The door on the skidder was locked, but the door on the log loader was open. Paul climbed into the cab and searched. He rummaged through the cab with no success. He sat in the seat, moved the levers as if operating the machine. The appeal of working a piece of equipment so much larger than his body was intoxicating. That extension of power was dangerous if a man was weak.

Paul left the worksite and walked back to his cabin on the family trail. The trail all the generations had trod down. The trail that once ran through the most beautiful part of the forest, the quietest part, the part Paul felt run through his blood and was closest to his heart. The memories, imperfectly imprinted, turned through his mind as his feet moved over this portion of earth his family claimed. A sickness rose in the back of Paul's throat as he reached the cabin, a sickness he fed with thoughts of revenge as he stood on the porch looking through the thin line of trees now separating his land from his cousin's.

Paul spent the next day trying to ignore the sounds of saws and falling trees. He harvested some kale, pulled a few carrots from the ground, cut some beet greens, and wondered what his damn cousin was going to buy with the blood money earned from the timber. Paul thought about what he was going to say at Thanksgiving before breaking his cousin's nose. He balled up his fist and looked at it. He was proud of the roughness of his hands, the way dirt lived in the cracks of his skin, the way a life of hard work had thickened his fingers and made his handshake something to be feared. He imagined his large fist mashing his cousin's soft Portland nose. "Maybe you can use that money to fix your face," that's what he'd say as he stood over his cousin.

In the afternoon, Paul was near the top of his property planting alder cuttings when all the noise from the job site stopped. The silence was sudden and jarring, and followed by men shouting. Paul started to walk toward the cacophony to get a better view through the narrow scrim of remaining trees but stopped once he saw the frantic movements of men trying to extricate one of the loggers from a tangle of logs and branches snarled on the forest floor.

Men in the heavy yellow machines moved the twisted mess as delicately as possible to free the trapped man. Paul sat watching.

When the man was finally released from the pine prison, the team of loggers carried him to the white truck, carefully placed him in the bed and held him as still as possible as they drove away from the worksite.

Silence returned to the forest.

Paul waited a few minutes before walking over to the calamitous spot to see what had happened.

The tangle of limbs made it difficult going, but eventually he arrived at the spot where the man had been trapped. The four yellow logging machines were still huddled around the mess.

There was no blood, nothing to indicate how badly the logger was injured.

He looked around the mess of brush and found a large chainsaw. He picked it up. It was heavier than his, the bar on the saw looked to be close to a yard long, and the engine was big and blocky; this was not a saw for weekenders. He put his right hand on the rear hand guard and flicked at the trigger throttle with his index finger. He lifted the saw with his left arm and moved it around in the imaginary motions of a logger.

Was he man enough to run a saw this size all day? He turned the saw, lifted it, and felt the muscles in his shoulders respond. As he moved, his eye caught a clear glimpse of the large cedar, his large cedar.

The majestic tree sat in the back corner of the cut, fully exposed, with two large red X's spray painted onto the bark. Emma's swing hung limply, the ropes traveled up into the canopy as if connected to heaven. Paul scanned the tree line; the red X's were almost all gone. His large cedar was being left for last.

Paul walked uphill about fifty feet to the eldest tree on the lot and stood in its shadow. One hundred years ago his great grandfather stood here wondering whether he should cut it down. Instead Paul's great grandfather left the cedar to grow into a future he would never know. He found the place where his great grandfather shaved the bark off the tree and carved his initials: JC. His grandfather's initials, his father's initials, his initials, everyone who ever lived on this land carved their initials into the same naked spot on the tree. Paul ran his fingers across the scars.

Something stirred in Paul as he turned to look down the hillside. He didn't believe in the nonsense of ancestors floating somewhere up there, watching over the living, but he repeated father's words, "Doin' it right means doin' it yourself." Those words breathed life into an idea and when Paul saw the hulking yellow machines gathered below, he fed the flames of the idea into motion.

Paul set the saw down at the base and stood next to the ancient cedar. He pressed his chest against the trunk and looked up into the sky. He looked at the branches to see which side had the most weight. He moved around the circumference like a silent dance partner.

From the base, it looked like most of the weight was on the downhill side. Years of sunlight and winds made the tree grow that way. He wrapped his arms around the trunk and held the tree for a moment. It swayed and groaned as the wind played with the treetop.

Paul picked up the saw. He flipped the kill switch, cranked the choke open, grabbed the front handle with his left hand, then gripped the plastic starter handle, lifted the saw engine to his chest, and in one smooth motion dropped the engine body with his left and pulled the handle and string with his right. The saw sputtered to life. Paul turned the choke off and squeezed the throttle trigger with his right index finger. The saw roared. Paul walked to the northern side of the tree, found the naked spot with his family's initials, tipped the saw so the bar was flat, dug the bumper spike into the tree to use as a pivot point an inch below the bare spot on the trunk, and let the teeth of the saw begin chewing into the large cedar.

The saw spit flakes of wet sawdust back at Paul in a shower. Paul squeezed the throttle and held it there as he cut the bottom of the wedge into the tree. He reset the pivot point several times and since the saw wasn't long enough to cut all the way through the trunk he moved to the south side to get a clean wedge cut into the tree.

The top of the wedge was a little more difficult because of the weight of the saw, but after twenty minutes of sweat and effort Paul kicked the wedge out of the tree, turned the saw off and picked up the heavy wedge.

He sat in his daughter's swing which had been his swing, and his father's swing, and held the wedge: an ancient artifact. Paul turned the wedge and looked at the initials of those who came before him.

He looked at the rings formed by years and years of growth. Each ring a solar year. Paul thought about the rain, about the sunlight, about the wind, and about what was happening while this tree sat on this piece of earth growing taller and taller. The rings closer to the edge were years when two twin towers fell, somewhere near the edge was the moonwalk and Kennedy assassinations, further along this tree survived the World Wars and the Civil War. Paul ran his finger across the years. He felt his impermanence and then stood up to finish his job.

He grabbed the saw and moved behind the tree. He fired the saw awake and began the back cut. The saw chewed through the years as it was designed to, spewing out the Reagan administration, the Great Depression, the signing of the Constitution...somewhere between the writing of *Hamlet* and the battle of Hastings the heart of the great tree snapped. The crack vibrated through the forest, the great tree leaned, tipped slowly and crashed down across the four hulking yellow machines below.

Paul hit the kill switch, set the saw on the oozing stump, picked up the wedge, and walked back to his cabin on the trail his great grandfather cut into the woods more than one hundred years ago.

Puget Sound Ferry Ride

After the security checks and various delays,
The boat moves away from the dock.
To the south, Rainier's snowcap floats above
The city, disconnected from its base.

Walking out on deck, the Sound's enfolding beauty
Whispers to my past.
From my omniscient view, I look into
The deep alongside the ferry and see.

Inside each wave is a smaller one, and
Inside those small waves are smaller waves.
Smaller and smaller each wave containing small worlds.
From distances, it all looks smooth and complete.

Earlier in the day I moved so close to Seurat's
The Models that I could see
The empty canvas beyond
The dots.

Has the world's great artist left any corner undone?
Each microscopic wave forms a great blue canvas.
If I could get close enough, could I see the brush strokes
And understand those whispers?

The Icelandic Phallological Museum

Warning: Formaldehyde causes shrinkage

When I heard that Reykjavik had its very own penis museum, I knew I had to visit. How else would anyone want to spend a sunny day in Iceland's only major city? While other people were out visiting the natural wonders of the Icelandic countryside, I was walking around (lost as usual) trying to find The Icelandic Phallological Museum.

I walked right by the front door. I guess I was expecting something to be sticking out into the street, but there wasn't anything to scream, "Look in here for penises!" When I finally decided to take out a map and look at an address, it took me to a building with no signage. I looked inside to see if the museum was hidden upstairs in some dark corner, but it wasn't.

It was right next door; I didn't realize the actual location until I walked across the street and then looked back at the building. There it was, the world's only penis museum, and if you know me, you know I love a good museum. So, I went back across the street and entered the museum as discretely as possible (nobody cares what you do in Iceland, it's like Vegas except colder, more expensive, and has more Russian gangsters. The guy at the tourist office told me that the penis museum was a must see).

The young lady at the counter took my 1,250 IK ($10) and gave me a little information. "This is an English explanation of all the penises in the museum. The little number corresponds to the specimens."

I didn't think I would need much help because...well, because every man in the world believes they know everything they need to know about penises. I soon found this was a myth (at least in my case; the rest of you can continue thinking you know everything about penises). I was glad I had the little guide because as soon as I turned the corner, I was confronted by...yikes!

Sperm Whales must be swimming in cold water to keep these six-footers hidden (all you biologists take a deep breath; I know that whales hide their fandangoruskies in a little, or big, pocket or something). The collection is primarily penises from Icelandic mammals. There are some foreign penises, but they had to get a visa to stay more than six months; not really, this is an immigration joke. I assume all the penises came from dead mammals.

There were a few interesting things in the museum, but the founder's story was the most entertaining. This museum wasn't some dream of his; he just started with a bull's penis whip. I guess there are whips made from bull penises. I have not seen one so I cannot be too certain.

Anyway, the guy started the museum when people he worked with started giving him penises as gifts. How one becomes known as the "penis gift guy" is not something I want to delve too deeply into, but let me just say that after a bit, he had quite a collection. Someone then suggested that he open a museum, and the rest is history, or as I like to think, "This guy needed an excuse to keep collecting, so a museum sounded like a good idea."

Penises of all shapes and sizes filled the tiny museum, including three from human donors, one English, one German and, not to let the home team down, one Icelander.

I did not look too closely and was a little surprised that they were actually there. I thought the museum was still looking for a human donor, but apparently not. Too bad guys, your dreams of donating your willy to a museum are now over. I don't think they are still in the market, but you can check the webpage.

My favorite part of the museum was just a bunch of stuff that looked like penises. Veggies, fruit, rocks, pieces of wood. They even had a mythology section where there were penises from trolls, gnomes, mermen, and ghosts.

The strangest thing in the whole museum was a little shrine to the Icelandic silver medal handball team. The little silver statues were created to celebrate the great success of the team, but the guys on the team were not consulted in the creation. In other words, the penises were imagined or fictionalized. I don't know if the handball team wore really tight spandex or if the artist just got inspired and followed his/her muse.

The penis museum did not disappoint. It had penises and penis-related items. I did not buy a T-Shirt but if you really want one, they are available at: www.phallus.is

Drift Treasures

Raymond's daily schedule was not complicated: wake up before sunrise, have one cup of Folgers, dress according to the weather, and walk the tip of Sandy Peninsula looking for drift treasure for his website DriftTreasures.com. Raymond had an eye for drift treasure, and his house was situated in the perfect location for finding bits of floating gold. Most people walked right by the really good stuff because they were amateurs, but Raymond's eye recognized dulled treasure amidst the tidal trash.

The Sandy Peninsula jutted out just enough to collect tidal debris from the North Pacific current as it met and mixed with the fresh water of the Evergreen River. The currents pushed and pulled at each other spitting up oddly shaped pieces of driftwood, glass bottles worn down by years of ocean travel, commercial fishing buoys, and truly odd things that somehow ended up in the ocean and were deposited close to Raymond's front door. The stranger the object the more Raymond could charge and the faster it would sell.

Like any wise businessman Raymond split his webpage into pages for wood, glass, plastic, buoys, oddities, and the most popular, Japanese Tsunami debris. Whether it really was

Tsunami debris or not was not important. If it looked Japanese, felt Japanese, and had that foreign boxy text printed somewhere on the treasure Raymond classified it as "Tsunami debris." He did include a disclaimer at the very bottom of the page in six-point font that read, "Buyer beware. Tsunami debris has not been verified." It wasn't like he was selling ancient art to the Getty; there was no provenance in drift treasures.

Each piece was photographed, priced, and described by size and weight on the website. Some days Raymond could get as many as five hundred visitors. With shipping, handling and the cost of each item, Raymond could pay for his existence. It wasn't much of an existence, but it was better than most high school dropouts could manage on their own.

The day that Raymond found the shoe was a cold and windy one. He stood at the kitchen window of his singlewide looking out at the tip of Sandy Peninsula sipping his Folgers, knowing that it was a full-Grundéns day: an orange Harvestor 44 jacket and Harvestor bib pants day. Gusts of wind tapped at the aluminum storm door of his trailer as he dressed. "Let's get those boots on," he said to himself bending down. "Where'd I leave the sack? Must be in the shed. Okay, Raymond, let's find some drift treasures." He stopped noticing that he talked to himself a few years back; maybe it was a way to keep him focused, but probably it was something larger than that.

When the flashlight beam hit the red shoe, he was still twenty feet from it. The early light had yet to reach Sandy Peninsula, so Raymond did not look at the basketball shoe too closely; he just picked it up, tossed it into his mesh bag and kept walking. It did feel heavy, but everything feels heavy when it has been in the ocean. It never occurred to Raymond that he should check to see if there was still a foot in the shoe, but who thinks to see if a drifting shoe has a foot in it?

Once he finished his morning route, sticking to the high tide line on the way out and along the shore on the way in, Raymond sorted the drift treasures in the three-sided wooden shed he built from four old pieces of 4x8 plywood. Raymond thought the little shed might blow over in the wind and dent his singlewide, but rain and ocean mist had swollen the plywood, so it weighed several hundred pounds, and it now had become an integral part of his operation. He plunked the heavy bag of goods on the plastic fold-up table and turned the work light on. He grabbed the bottom corners of the sack and emptied the drift treasures onto the table. His gut told him that the basketball shoe might be the best bit of treasure this morning, so he pushed aside the wood, the glass bottles and saw the sole of the shoe: Air Jordan. Raymond pulled it out of the pile. Instinctively he turned the shoe over to see if a hermit crab had made this place his home. Much to Raymond's surprise there was no crab, but there was a severed foot.

Raymond dropped the shoe on the table and backed away. Taking a few deep breathes Raymond considered his options: toss the thing back in the ocean, call the sheriff, cut the laces and open the shoe to see if the whole foot was there.

An ordinary man might not be as curious as Raymond, or an ordinary man might not want to see a severed foot, but Raymond was curious, and he did want to see a severed foot.

When Sheriff Johnson arrived, the sun was up, and he was not happy. Raymond showed him the shoe and the foot, and the sheriff just shook his head. "What the hell were you thinking, son? Why didn't you just leave it on the beach?"

"I don't know."

"Why'd you take the foot out of the shoe?"

"I wanted to see what it looked like."

"That was just damn irresponsible. How'd you get it out of the shoe?"

"I took my Leatherman and cut the laces." Raymond made an upward motion with his right hand. "I held the shoe with those barbeque tongs, and then I just turned it over and shook it out."

"Geez, son. I don't know what to say. Don'tcha watch any of them CSI shows? Don'tcha know to leave evidence alone?"

"I didn't know it was evidence, I thought it was just a drift treasure."

"Drift treasure? Detached feet aren't treasure, that's feet. That's somebody's foot. People don't just toss these things into the sea." Sheriff Johnson shook his head, "Alright. Anything else you want to let me know?"

"The foot is kind of green, but the skin isn't puckered at all. Do you think that is a clue?"

"Nope, I don't think that is much of a clue. If we threw you in the water for a week you'd turn green."

"But wouldn't my skin pucker?"

"Hell, I don't know," the sheriff said tossing his hands in the air. "I guess so. Usually when we find bodies they are pretty puckered up, so maybe it is a clue, but we usually don't have to convince people not to play with dead body parts." Sheriff Johnson turned around and looked down toward the beach, "Well, show me where you found it."

"I don't remember."

"You don't remember? I would think that finding a severed human foot would be something you would remember."

"Yeah, but I don't remember. I just picked it up and kept going."

"Son, how stupid do you think I am? You expect me to believe that you just found this foot on the beach and you didn't notice?"

"It's the truth."

The sheriff made a long grumbling noise in the back of his throat and shook his head. "Well, show me where you think you found it. Maybe the rest of this guy is out there somewhere."

"Okay."

The two men walked slowly along the high tide line as Raymond did his best to recreate his morning. Remembering things had never been Raymond's strength, even before the incident with Ryan Iverson at the Local Tavern, but now it was even more difficult to recall tiny details. The daily seizures had gone away, but every now and again, when a storm passed through, he felt the sensation in the back of his head like a little ball of electricity waiting to explode.

Raymond led the sheriff through the routine: walk out along the high tide line and walk back along the water. There wasn't anything to find. Raymond knew once the sun was up all the good stuff disappeared; life worked that way.

By the time the two men got back to the shed, Sheriff Johnson had given up on the case. He put the shoe in a large zip-lock bag, put the foot in a different bag, tossed the two bags in the trunk and before backing out of Raymond's driveway, rolled down the window, "Raymond, if you find anything else out there, leave it alone. Call me first."

"Okay, I will," Raymond said, "Hey, Sheriff will I get the shoe back? It's probably worth a lot on my website."

"You know what, I don't know. I assume there was a crime, but maybe some poor fisherman just lost a foot. Hey, if nobody shows up to claim it and there isn't a crime within ninety days, you can come and get it."

It was the worst thing the Sheriff could have said to Raymond.

While Sheriff Johnson was busy filling out his report and double bagging the foot, Raymond was out walking the Sandy Peninsula again. Raymond's rubber boots scrunched through the heavy sand as he walked the shoreline not looking at the ground, but at the rolling, dark water of the Pacific. Somewhere out there was nine-tenths of a man. Somewhere out there was another red sized-twelve Air Jordan attached to a left foot. "It must be out there," Raymond whispered to himself as he walked the loose sand.

The next three mornings Raymond waited for the sun to rise before having his Folgers. He walked the peninsula but didn't pick up any drift treasures. In the evening, he skipped watching *Entertainment Tonight* and walked the beach instead. He found nothing. The sun set and Raymond decided to give up his quest.

The following morning, he was up early with his cup of Folgers. He looked into the darkness preparing himself for the cold. He slipped into his work clothing, grabbed his mesh bag, and trudged onto the wet sand. His flashlight scanned the sloped beach for anything the tide had dragged up from the depths and deposited on his shore. On the way out, along the high tide line, he found a few interesting pieces of driftwood, a green Russian glass buoy, a few plastic bottles that looked like they had Japanese writing on them, and a small bicycle tire from a child's trike.

As he turned to come back, Raymond noticed the sunrise filling the sky with fuming red colors swirling around a thick mass of menacing clouds. He walked along the shoreline but lost focus. Instead of scanning the wet sand in front of him, he found himself looking out into the black water as it pulled by the peninsula. The waves heaved and pitched, shining, and darkening as they rolled. He imagined all that was hidden beneath those black waters: the shipwrecked boats, the great cedar trees that had lost their battle with the Pacific, and the bodies of sailors long since forgotten.

Then Raymond saw something, something red. It might have been a reflection, but it disappeared as the wave dipped. Raymond stood still. He knew any movement would change his perspective and he would lose the location of the object. He waited. He waited for the light and the rise of the wave to cooperate, and then they did. There was something there, one hundred feet offshore where the ebb and flow of the tide met. Maybe it was the light, maybe it was Raymond's imagination creating more than was there, but it looked to Raymond like the body of a man. Raymond walked ten feet up shore and scratched out a large arrow in the sand pointing toward the floating body.

He scrambled up the beach to his trailer. He didn't bother pulling off his boots as he hopped inside and grabbed his binoculars. He orientated the lenses, found the sand arrow and moved over the water as carefully as he could. The tide was going out, so he did his best to take into account the moving water. His sharp eyes, trained to find the unusual, to find the odd, to pick the single out of the many, scanned the moving water.

The rising sun, the rolling water, Raymond's shaking hands, all conspired to hide the drift treasure that he knew was there. Further and further from shore Raymond looked until, at the mouth of the harbor, he saw it again: a body dressed in blue jeans with one red shoe.

He dropped the binoculars on the window seat and ran outside. He reached beneath his trailer and dragged out his 12-foot rowboat. Raymond pulled the boat through the beach grass, over the dry sand and down to the lapping water. He eased the skiff into the waves and began pulling with both oars. The chop slapped against the bow of the tiny craft, but since the tide was going out Raymond was moving rapidly.

Maybe it was the first gust of wind, or maybe it was the first wave to break over the bow of the boat, but something reminded Raymond that he had taken the life-vest out of the boat before fall and put it inside his trailer so it wouldn't get moldy. It was a memory that would have sent a less curious man back to shore.

Raymond rested for a moment. He could see the mouth of the harbor just ahead. He watched the waves toss and pitch wildly as the wind blew gusts of foam across the surface. His little boat could capsize, but it could also be small enough that he would skim across the surface and be perfectly safe.

Raymond waited. He felt the water swell and drop. He felt the sting of the salty spray. He felt the tiny ball of electricity building in the back of his head. He felt small. "I'll get that body and then who will be the irresponsible one," Raymond said as he turned his back on the turbulent water, looked out at the boiling red horizon, and pulled toward the open ocean.

***

When the autopsy was complete and all the tests were in, the coroner determined that the cause of death was drowning. There was no way to determine if drugs or alcohol were involved because the body had been in the water for at least a week when a local found him washed up on the shore. No one was certain why a man who could not swim would take his small rowboat out past the harbor bar in conditions that were not ideal, but Raymond had always been a strange fellow and his death, although unexplained, seemed like the logical end for someone who made a living from drift treasures.

ACKNOWLEDGEMENTS

Thank you:

Linda B. Myers, Heidi Hansen, and Melee VanderVelde
Dana and Kim Minard
Sequim Writers Group: Lisa Corbit, Patrick Benapfl, Sarah
Shepherd, and Alana Baxter
Rainshadow Poetry
Olympic Theatre Arts for Story Slam and book launch
Fourth Friday Readings Group
Olympic Peninsula Authors
Peter Gallo in Westport
Barbara Bachelor in Westport
Whitworth College: MAC Hall with Eric Henrickson
Kenyon College in Ohio for Keats and Wordsworth
Ocosta School District (Teachers, Students)
Port Angeles School District (Teachers, Students)
Sequim School District (Teachers, Students)
David and Geri Eekhoff (Dad and Mom)
Kay, Jenni, and Mike (Sisters, Brother)
University of Washington Speech and Hearing Clinic
Harborview Hospital Seattle (everyone who works there)
Olympic Medical Center
Clallam County Fire Department paramedics
And whoever paid for my trip from Olympic Medical Center to
Harborview

Geanie.
425 219 9772.
6/6/23 CARE GIVER

Made in the USA
Monee, IL
21 February 2022